(1N6)

3/05

(1N6)

The Groom's Guide

ALSO BY SHARON NAYLOR

The Mother-of-the-Bride Book

The New Honeymoon Planner

The Complete Outdoor Wedding Planner

The Ultimate Bridal Shower Idea Book

Your Special Wedding Vows

Your Special Wedding Toasts

How to Have a Fabulous Wedding for $10,000 or Less

How to Plan an Elegant Wedding in 6 Months or Less

1001 Ways to Have a Dazzling Second Wedding

*Your Day, Your Way: The Essential Handbook
    for the 21st Century Bride*
    (co-written with celebrity bridal gown designers
    Michelle Roth and Henry Roth)

The Groom's Guide

A Wedding Planner for Today's Marrying Man

Sharon Naylor

CITADEL PRESS
Kensington Publishing Corp.
www.kensingtonbooks.com

CITADEL PRESS books are published by

Kensington Publishing Corp.
850 Third Avenue
New York, NY 10022

All Kensington titles, imprints, and distributed lines are available at special quantity discounts for bulk purchases for sales promotions, premiums, fund raising, educational, or institutional use. Special book excerpts or customized printings can also be created to fit specific needs. For details, write or phone the office of the Kensington special sales manager: Kensington Publishing Corp., 850 Third Avenue, New York, NY 10022, attn: Special Sales Department; phone 1-800-221-2647.

First printing: September 2004

10   9   8   7   6   5   4   3   2   1

Printed in the United States of America

Library of Congress Control Number: 2004106003

ISBN 0-8065-2595-9

For Madison and Kevin

ACKNOWLEDGMENTS

WITH MANY THANKS to my editor Bruce Bender from Kensington Books and my literary agent Meredith Bernstein for bringing this project to the table.

And with gratitude to those who shared their expertise and their real-life stories: Todd and Krista Meikle of WedStudio.com, Janet Holian of VistaPrint.com, Meredith Vellines of Schwartz Communication, Leslie Vismara of VismaraInvitations.com, Steve Blahitka of Back East Productions, and the many marrying couples from across the country who shared their stories with me.

As always, a big thank you to my family and friends . . .

Contents

III: The Big Moments

IV: After the Wedding

Preface

WELL, YOU DID IT. . . . You slipped that sparkling ring on her finger, asked the question she's been dying to hear (hopefully, you heard yourself above the sound of your pounding heart), and now you're an engaged man! Champagne corks popped, onlookers may have applauded you, and the love of your life is burning up her cell-phone minutes calling everyone she knows to tell the story of *how you did it*.

While your buddies might be rolling their eyes, slapping their foreheads with something along the lines of "There goes another one!" and maybe even collecting some cash on their bets over your matrimonial fate, you can forget about the scary soundtrack and the ball-and-chain mentality that grooms of yesteryear boasted. Today's groom, the twenty-first-century groom, is not quite so cynical. Okay, so perhaps you'd rather dig out your own spleen with a spoon than spend hours flipping through a big, fat, glossy bridal magazine with your wedding-buzzed bride-to-be, but you're probably excited about *some* parts of the wedding plans. After all, 80 percent of today's grooms are involved as full partners in the wedding plans, and they're not afraid to say it.

> *I don't want to be a guest at my own wedding. I might not have walked into this whole thing with thirty years of wedding fantasies in my head like my fiancée did, but I definitely know what I want and what I don't want at my wedding. The day is about US, not just her, and I don't want my buddies eating canapés and listening to harp music the whole time.*
>
> —Brian, 29, from Boston

We're paying for the wedding, so you're darn straight I'm going to be a part of planning it. Not just to keep the spending in line, but I really do want to put together a great party where all of my friends will feel comfortable.

—Michael, 33, from Orlando

Marriage is important to us, and to my family. My parents have been married for thirty-six years, and I value the importance of celebrating commitment. So I'm fully focused on creating a ceremony that reflects our promises, our faith, and even our cultural backgrounds. It's not just about the reception . . . it's about the larger reason for being there in the first place: that we love each other and want to build a life together.

—Seth, 28, from Oakland

Make no mistake, today's grooms—and that includes you—take their weddings seriously, and their brides are happy to share the entire process with them. Decades ago, the groom's involvement was attending the engagement party, renting a tuxedo, and showing up on time for the ceremony. Now grooms are fully immersed in the following favorite tasks for the man of the hour:

- Choosing the entertainment (That means going out to see bands in live performance and auditioning them privately.)
- Setting up wedding Web sites (Anything having to do with the computer is a big draw for today's groom.)
- Hiring the photographer and videographer (Anything having to do with technology is *hot* with grooms, especially since today's weddings involve more technology than ever before.)
- Choosing the limousines or classic cars (When else will you ever be driven around in a car that costs more than your mortgage down payment?)

- ◆ Planning the menu and bar lists (Because we know you love your food your way, and you probably know your favorite wines and liquors too.)
- ◆ Planning the honeymoon (Run away to a private island, cruise to Alaska, scuba dive off the Great Barrier Reef—the great getaway plans are in your hands as well, and the trends in honeymoons are moving to more adventure and more exotic locales.)

So your bride is not the only one with the full To Do list here. Since I know you're a busy man, I've collected everything you need to know about the wedding business, the questions you need to ask, the tiny details that might fly by you if you're not careful, and the grand gestures and little extra somethings you can plan to impress your bride . . . and your future in-laws. Wedding planning is not a woman's world anymore . . . it's also your world now, and you're free to select whichever tasks you'd like to handle on your own or in tandem with your fiancée.

Please note that this book is interactive as well. If you have any questions about anything you read here, or any issues that crop up while making your wedding plans, you can access me directly through my Web site, www.sharonnaylor. net, and I will give you personal guidance. The wedding industry is a 3.2-billion-dollar one, and you'll discover as you go along that it can be quite a confusing and detailed road you're on. You're about to discover what besom pockets are, where stephanotis is grown, and the difference between wedding insurance and special event insurance. It's enough to make your head spin.

You have this book to guide you through the planning details, and—perhaps most important—how to *work with your bride, and with her family* in what you'll soon learn is the most emotionally and diplomatically charged time of your life. Weddings make even quite well-adjusted people slightly insane, and in some cases certifiable. With so many details and so much outside influence from relatives and vendors who might need to take a crash course in social skills and discretion, things can get hairy quickly. And you'll be at the center of it all, taking turns as the hero of the day, counselor, shoulder to cry on, celebrant, and all around high-style guy.

You're going to be measured and tested, and at every step of the way you'll be preparing not just for the wedding day but for life after the wedding. This is where it all begins, where you and your bride join hands in this big, sentimental (and expensive!) task, and learn more about what you're both made of and what kind of couple you are. And you thought it was just about choosing a tux, a bouquet, a meal, and a band!

Get the message now: weddings are serious business and emotional roller-coasters, all to get you to the point of being married.

And now you're on your way . . .

Take notes. Learn from what my spotlight grooms in this book have to say, and enjoy the ride. Because if you do it right, this is the only time you'll ever have to go through planning a wedding. So make it fun, make it a working partnership with your bride, and remember to make it all about the two of you and just what you mean to each other.

Ready? Now let's get started. . . .

I

The Basics

I

◇ ◇ ◇

What Kind of Wedding
Do You Want?

"What kind of wedding do I want? Does it matter?"

ACTUALLY, YES. It does. While you might think you're out of the loop on the whole wedding-vision thing, you do have a say in the matter. Sure, when your bride bats her eyelashes and asks, "What do you think, honey?" she might just want you to volley back an agreement with whatever she has in mind—that way you're technically involved without screwing up her own well-entrenched wedding designs. Many women have ways of asking these kinds of loaded questions, you know . . .

But let's just focus on today's bigger and more common picture—that your bride really *does* want your input right here at the beginning, that it really *is* a joint decision. This is where you both sit down and put pen to paper, making the first big decisions that set the foundation for your big day.

Your very first topic to tackle is the style and size of your wedding. We'll get to size in a moment, because size *does* matter when it comes to weddings. (Everything from the budget to the location to many more of your decisions will depend on whether you have a fifty-person guest list or the more common one hundred fifty.) For now, we're looking at the style of your impending wedding celebration. Let me ask you . . .

3

Do you see yourself in a tuxedo at an ultraformal affair, escorting your bride into a lavish ballroom dripping with crystal and awash in a sea of white-rose floral arrangements? An orchestra or band is playing, your guests are dressed in their finest, and waiters are presenting canapés and flutes of champagne on silver platters? Do you see yourself at this high-style, five-star event, or . . .

Do you see yourself on the beach in Maui with a lei around your neck, and your bride approaching in a white bikini top and a white sarong, with a hibiscus tucked behind her ear? Your guests are barefoot on the beach in sundresses or short-sleeved shirts and khaki shorts, a steel-drum band plays in the background, and sunscreen is your chosen accessory for the day?

What's it going to be? High-style and top-shelf or laid-back and surf's-up? I've chosen the two most diverse examples to give you an idea of the range you have open to you. In the middle, you can choose among the following examples:

- A big, tented outdoor wedding on the lawn of a historic estate or arboretum
- A formal wedding outside by the pool at a beautiful hotel
- A more informal backyard gathering with all the kids invited
- A semiformal ballroom reception in the afternoon
- A theme wedding, perhaps a 1920s Great Gatsby look, a Moroccan escapade, a seaside ocean-theme . . .
- An ethnic wedding that's culturally diverse and blends both your backgrounds
- A formal dessert-and-champagne-only reception held in the late evening hours
- A laid-back brunch on a Sunday afternoon
- A small, but formal, reception in the tasting room at a winery with fine wines, cheeses, and tasty hot hors d'oeuvres on the menu
- A completely unique and surprising event, like the underwater scuba-diving wedding or the hot-air-balloon ceremony held high above the mountains or vineyards, where you land to the applause of your guests and then proceed to the reception nearby
- Last, but never least, the "Let's just take off to Vegas" wedding

Weddings are no longer one-size-fits-all, and you might be surprised to find out that your fiancée is one of the millions of future brides out there who wants to break out of tradition, not have the same formal wedding all of her friends are having, get really creative and unique, and plan a wedding that's more *the two of you* than the status quo. We in the wedding industry are seeing a huge trend in taking that traditional wedding mold and smashing it to bits in favor of a way-more-personalized celebration from start to finish. So you'll be happy to know that you *can* play with the formal wedding and add fun, creative, even quirky touches.

Don't Think Money Yet

I have to stop you right here to get that big dollar sign out of your head for now. Of course, the issue of money and "What Is This Going to Cost?" is ever-present when you're talking weddings: money is the proverbial three-headed beast that can add an incredible amount of stress to the entire process. Yes, money is a controlling factor, but right now it is *not* your deciding factor. If you start here thinking, "Now which of these styles would be less expensive?" and opt for that one, you're making a big mistake. Because *none* of these styles of weddings are, by rule, more or less expensive than the others. Money is not a deciding factor for style. You can plan a $20,000 super-formal wedding at a hotel or a $50,000 outdoor wedding. You can spend $5,000 to run off to Tahiti for a destination wedding, or $50,000 on an all-family-invited wedding in your backyard. Any style can be had at any price, depending on the size of it plus your individual spending choices like location, menu, décor, and so on. So money, when it comes to style, isn't the only factor. The style you want can be yours. Nothing gets ruled out at this point.

So, What Elements Say *You* as a Couple?

Your starting point here is going to be as simple as thinking about what's *you*. For many couples, there's no question. They got engaged on the beach at sunset, so it's going to be a beach wedding, perhaps at the same stretch of beach where she said yes loud enough to scare the seagulls away. If you're the formal, traditional types, then you might simply agree on the beautiful, lavish traditional wedding, but with a pop of customizing in the cocktail hour (where you'll have a special drink or food choice on the menu, like the mashed potato bar one groom requested, or Japanese string music playing in the background).

Before you go any further, take some time to sit down with your fiancée and brainstorm. What is truly *you*? Is there a theme that you both would love? Are there *elements* of a theme that you can weave into your day? Do you have special moments in mind, like drinking a toast with your bride at sunset?

It's All in the Size

Obviously, there's going to be a big difference in scope and price tag for a formal wedding with fifty guests invited versus one with two hundred fifty guests. That's a no-brainer. The size issue is perhaps the biggest factor when you're considering the style and formality of your wedding. Not only do you have to factor in the per-person costs in feeding and hosting each guest, your total guest head count may very well determine *where* you'll hold your wedding. That giant ballroom at the Four Seasons would be ideal for your two-hundred-plus guest list, while a smaller but equally elegant party room or beachside restaurant's outdoor terrace would suit your seventy-five-person guest list. The prices work accordingly. It may be simple math, but it is something that many couples don't think to consider right off the bat.

So, right here is where you start sketching out just *how big* a wedding you want. Do the two of you want to invite everyone you've ever known? Or do you want to keep it to immediate family and close friends? What about your parents? If they're kicking in for the planning and paying for the wedding, will they have guests of their own whom they'd like to invite? Do you have international friends who might be able to come? What about guests' kids? Who is going to share the big day with you?

My best advice about this initial guest list head count is to *create tiers*, assigning levels of "importance" to the guests on your list. I know, it's bad form to assign ranking numbers to your nearest and dearest, but trust me on this. When it comes time to create your realistic, actual guest list down the road a bit, you're going to thank me.

You'll create tiers according to a model like this:

Tier 1: Parents, grandparents, siblings, godparents, guardians, stepparents, and your own children, if applicable. These are the people you consider Must Have's, without question.

Tier 2: Your closest friends, some being like family to you.

Tier 3: Aunts and uncles, great-aunts and great-uncles, first cousins, colleagues, and additional friends—people you definitely want on your guest list.

Tier 4: Additional colleagues, clients, neighbors, distant relatives, friends of the family.

Tier 5: Your parents' friends, your siblings' friends, and so on—people who get invited only if there's plenty of room.

With your guests' names assigned to these tiers—perhaps organized on a workable computer spreadsheet—you'll have a much more organized way to "cut" guests from the list once you know what your budget and space allowances will be for the wedding site you choose. With one chop, you eliminate everyone from Tier 5, for instance. This is a particularly good way to organize your guest head count to keep you in range when you're looking for wedding day locations and starting to look at price packages.

I don't mean to sound incredibly impersonal when it comes to "ranking" and "chopping" friends and family. But this is the best way I've found to get ballpark numbers at this stage.

Are you getting the picture yet that the mini-details and "What If?" possibilities come into play when you're planning a wedding? Would you ever have

Special Friends, Special Family, Special Circumstances

When you're looking at your guest list with an aim toward figuring out your ideal wedding style and scope, remember to keep any special needs of your guests in mind. You might have elderly guests or a relative who uses a wheelchair. You might have a large number of guests who need to fly great distances to get to the wedding. It's important to be mindful of these special limitations when designing your wedding vision. For instance, one couple wrote in to say they regretted planning their wedding on a beach where guests had to walk through a wooded area to access the cove where the ceremony would take place. Their elderly guests had a lot of trouble walking that path and some required assistance. One refused to walk through the woods and needed to be driven a roundabout way to the site. Even if this kind of forethought seems like too much attention to detail, I assure you that guest sensitivities will be an issue. So it's best to take them into account when you're looking at an alternative location or wedding style like an outdoor, beach, or boat wedding. Will your guests be able (and be happy) to be there? One couple reconsidered their wishes for a cliffside wedding when they thought about all the little children who would be invited. The bride and groom knew they'd worry too much about inadequate child supervision and the complete lack of safety rails there, so they chose a beachside bluff instead. Same sunset, more safety, more peace of mind.

thought about whether or not your grandmother could step over tree roots and walk around mud puddles to get to your wedding site? These are the tight-focus details that might not even enter your consciousness at this stage, but as you'll see along the way, they will have a significant impact on your plans. It's these unique worries that build up to meltdown stage during the months of planning. So choose wisely now, delve into the full picture of each style you're considering, and you can avoid the trickiest of situations.

When Is This Going Down?

Very important to planning the style of your wedding is the *season* of your marriage, so look at the calendar now. That outdoor wedding, obviously, will need great weather, less of a chance of rain, maybe even beautiful fall foliage on the trees surrounding your reception site. If you're going with January, then you have the makings for a lavish winter wedding. June, and all options are open to you, both indoors and out. A Valentine's Day wedding might be your bride's romantic fantasy, with a sea of red roses as your décor and an anniversary date you won't forget (well, probably not).

The season of your wedding is important to your chosen style range, and *also to your budget*. While I said earlier that no one wedding style is inherently more or less expensive than another when all those selective details are added up, you will find that wedding services and packages *in general* will be higher priced during peak wedding season. Depending on where you live in the country, peak wedding season is usually somewhere between June and September; these are the most popular months for weddings due to the great weather and families' significantly more open schedules (i.e., the kids are out of school, so we can travel to your big event). Right now, July and August are the hot, hot months for weddings, with September and October picking up in popularity. But overall, you can expect big-time supply-and-demand prices during those peak months.

Couples who are looking to plan a wedding for less are often urged to plan *outside* of these peak wedding months in order to get a sizable percentage discount in their wedding professional's planning packages, and you'll find that a greater number of florists, caterers, photographers, bands, and so on, have more weekends available in March, April, and November. Those are considered off-peak months, and thus might be a good option for you.

How Long an Engagement Will This Be?

How much time would you both need in order to plan the wedding with as little rush as possible? Ideally, you'll set your wedding date for at least nine months to a year out. That's the best way to be sure you can find the best wedding professionals with dates available, and the best way to allow yourselves plenty of time

Be Aware!

When you're choosing your top three ideal wedding weekends—pick three for now in order to see which ceremony and reception sites have coordinating time slots open for you—make sure that you're not going to be crashing someone else's big event. Like a family reunion, another wedding in the family, or a child's birthday (they hate that!). See if the weekend you have in mind is going to be tough to swing for your closest relatives and friends; for instance, will your sister be taking the bar exam or her medical boards that week? Are your best friends scheduled to be on their own honeymoon at the time? Do some calling around to be sure that all your key players would be able to make it to your wedding, *especially* if you're planning a destination wedding and requiring them to travel with you. Other date issues to keep in mind when considering the availabilities of your guests:

- Vacation time: If the kids will be out of school, does your brother already have a vacation planned to Disney World?
- Guests' work schedules: Are you marrying during the weeks preceding tax time? If so, will your accountant friends be able to get out of the office for the weekend?
- Is it a holiday weekend?: Guests might not want to hit the road during heavy-traffic times such as Labor Day or Memorial Day. Also, is it the weekend *after* a holiday weekend? If you're looking at the weekend after Thanksgiving, know if most of your guests have just traveled far and wide to spend the holiday with their far-flung families; will they be okay about traveling yet again to get to your big event?

Sure, these are not make-or-break issues when it comes to planning your wedding date. Your friends and family are probably likely to hop in the car no matter which holiday is close to your wedding date, but I mention it here with a nod toward just considering which weekends might be more manageable for your most-valued guests. That makes you both gracious hosts, and it cuts down on the stress for everyone . . . yourselves included.

to make all the plans with at least a bit less stress. The one- or two-year engagement is more the norm among marrying couples, but you might find yourselves with a great window of opportunity six months from now. For instance, you might get engaged in the winter and wish to marry in the upcoming summer or fall. It's all do-able, provided you have the time in your schedules to devote to the planning. So figure out right now exactly *when* you'd like to take your trip down the aisle.

On the Web

Not sure if there's going to be a big tourism rush in the city where you'll be marrying? Check www.festivals.com to see if there's a cultural or sporting event planned for that town on that weekend. And call the town's board of tourism to find out about big conferences or conventions that will take place then too. While the bridesmaids might be thrilled about that firemen's convention in the hotel, your buddies might not want the competition.

One additional note about timing your wedding. It goes without saying that you should avoid the weekends of any sports play offs, the Super Bowl, NASCAR races, and also any big events in the city where you will marry. The first, because you don't want your guests (and you!) groaning that you have to miss the big game. Super Bowl weekend is perhaps the *least* popular weekend for weddings, making it the most popular weekend for bride-packed wedding expos and shows over at the hotel in town. Plan your wedding for the weekend of the Masters Tournament in Augusta, and you might find that many of your guests are either watching little TVs at their tables instead of dancing the tarantella with you, or they're all out at the bar and lounge area watching on the big-screen TV while you're cutting your wedding cake. Believe it or not, I'm a big sports fan too, and there's no way I'd ever hold my wedding during the play offs or the Super Bowl, the Masters, or any game that Derek Jeter is playing in. Some things just come first.

Beyond sports, you'll also need to know if the weekend of your wedding is going to be a *big* tourism weekend in the city where you will marry. If that great seaside town where your beach wedding will be held is likely to be overrun with spring breakers, then you'll face some unwanted wedding weekend scenarios. The town will be packed, prices for hotel rooms, food, gas, and entertainment there will skyrocket, causing extra financial hardship for you and for your guests. Restaurants could be jammed. Hotels could even be all booked for the summer. So consider the tourism factor for your location, and try to choose a location-specific date that's more open.

Get Your Priorities in Line

Right now—while you're enjoying a glass of merlot or cup of coffee with your bride-to-be, and while you're discussing your ideal type, size, and season of wedding—is the *perfect* time to start writing out your list of top priorities or individual wishes for the wedding. By this, I mean organizing your thoughts on paper about the things you both see as Must Haves for your wedding day. For instance, you both might feel strongly about marrying in your hometown. Or having a band versus a deejay. You both might want a beach wedding or a choir singing at your ceremony . . . or to be married in your church and not your parents'. From the big issues to the small, if there's something that's sacred to your wedding day wishes, this is the time to make it known and clear.

Pretty soon, you might have parents getting into the mix, whether or not they're official hosts or paying for even part of the wedding. And if that happens, you're going to find another whirlwind of details coming at you. Having a list of your firm wishes in hand is a way to make sure you're holding on to your highest priorities when things start getting more intense. Look at this sample list of absolute priorities for a model couple we'll call Mike and Lisa:

Mike and Lisa's Top Wedding Priorities
- Mike and Lisa want to marry in their parents' hometown of San Francisco
- Mike and Lisa want to get married outside of the church in an outdoor ceremony

Time-Saver

Go through the budget list worksheet in this book, and make a photocopy of it. Next to each item listed on that sheet, note the items that are your top priorities, and give them a ranking, such as $$$$$ for "This is so important to us, we're spending top dollar to have it," or $$$ for "We want this, but it's not a must-have," or X for "We can live without it." With all that arises during the planning of a wedding, at least you have your eye on your top wishes, no questions asked, and other helpers can also see in black and white that there are some areas where you're not willing to budge.

- ◆ Mike wants his father as his best man
- ◆ Lisa wants a designer gown
- ◆ Mike and Lisa want a formal reception with an Asian-theme cocktail hour to start

For now, that's their priority list. It will stand as firm. Later, when Lisa's mother chimes in with wanting her to marry in the church where *she* married, well, that's not possible. But Lisa is willing to give her mother some leeway on the décor plans, which are not as important to Lisa. And that's how having your top-priority list right there can save you a ton of trouble.

A Final Word on Designing the Wedding You Both Want

From moment one, keep in mind that your wedding plans are always fluid. Keeping a flexible and open mind about the wedding plans is the best way to prevent this process from knocking the two of you over, causing friction with families, and making this all a complete nightmare. In the world of weddings, things can change in a heartbeat, either because of a wedding professional's schedule, a seasonal snafu, or your own change of mind. So be open to the unexpected, because you're going to experience at least some . . . perhaps plenty. It's the couples who lock their knees and depend on certainties who get the worst of the process. If you stay open to tweaks and changes in your plans, even welcome them, I promise you a far better experience.

Vow to communicate well with one another right from the start, and by all means let your bride know right now—I mean *right now*—just how much input you want to have on a daily basis, just how much you want to be consulted. It's important to make everything clear so that her expectations don't become a problem for either of you. Set the ground rules now not only for the style of wedding you want, but for how the two of you are actually going to partner up throughout the process. I've devoted an entire chapter later on in this book on working with your bride through the highs and lows of planning a wedding, but I wanted to give you this timely advice (and warning): When you're setting the foundation of your wedding plans, you also need to set the foundation for your wedding-planning partnership. Now is a good time to discuss this. Pour another glass of merlot or heat up that coffee, and figure out the rules. There is no better start to this monumental effort.

Bringing in a Professional

You and your bride might wisely decide that you're way too busy with work and the workings of your lives to devote endless hours to the wedding plans, so you might wish to hire a wedding coordinator. So many couples are hiring a pro to do the research and present the best options, and they say it's a great investment and a big relief to be free of the dirty work (and the worrying). If this sounds like the two of you, start your search for a great wedding coordinator to plan everything from A to Z, or just to take over certain parts of the planning process, from finding a great site for your reception to scouting out the top three contenders for photography and videography. Log on to the Association of Bridal Consultants at www.bridalassn.com or the International Special Event Society at www.ises.com in order to find qualified pros to help you . . . or ask a recently married friend who he or she used.

2

◇ ◇ ◇

What's All This Going to Cost?

EVEN I HAVE A HARD TIME justifying spending upward of $40,000 on a *one-day celebration*, when that money would help out with a nice down payment on a house, so I can understand when marrying couples look at that national average and their jaws drop. In the United States, the average wedding budget is anywhere from $20,000 to $40,000. That's a lot of dough, especially these days, but the consensus among future and recent-past brides and grooms is that the investment is worth every penny. You can't put a price tag on the meaning and sentimentality of your wedding, especially your bride's attachment to the importance of the whole event. On the big day, most couples slip into a state of money amnesia, and it all becomes well worth those charred credit cards.

But you have a while to go before the money issue is clouded over by the significance of the big day. Right now, it's dollar signs on paper, and the high-roller numbers can weaken your knees. In some areas of the country, it's pretty common to see $125 to $150 charges *per guest* for just the reception. (So if you only want ten people at your wedding, you won't even blink.) You might come across $100 charges for *each* floral centerpiece, if not more in the neighborhood of $150 each (again, fine for that one table of ten guests). The figures can be staggering, but that's the beauty of the $3.2 billion wedding industry. They have you right where they want you, and they assume you'll pay top dollar to realize your wedding vision. This is a once-in-a-lifetime day for you, so they count on your throwing your self-control to the wind and whipping out your wallet to make the radiant bride even more radiant when she can have those gardenia and rose centerpieces with the imported stephanotis and lily of the valley. You wouldn't want to insult her by choosing everyday flowers, right?

Welcome to the wonderful financial world of weddings, where the price of everything bridal gets jacked up. Slap on some sentiment, and watch the prices go even higher. Before you take that guest list of yours and cross off Tiers 2 through 6, leaving only that one table of ten guests, take heart. There are ways of getting twice, even three times, the wedding for what you spend. In every area of wedding planning, all it takes is learning the language of that particular industry (flowers, photography, videography, catering, tuxes, and so on), asking the right questions, wheeling and dealing a little to slash your expenses *without sacrificing quality*. If there's one thing you take away from this book, I hope it's this: Never rip yourself off by cutting too deep to save money. Don't take the cheapo road, and don't leave out any of your most wished-for elements for the sake of cash. I promise you, both you and your bride will regret any extreme moves you make in order to save money. And you will regret walking into your reception with those shortcuts blaring like traffic signals to all of your guests that you planned a budget wedding. As great as you both look, your guests will see exactly where you cheaped out. And that's a big wedding faux pas that uninformed brides and grooms make. You're not going to make that mistake, because you have this book in your hands. Throughout this book, as promised earlier, I'm going to give you some pointers on classy, stylish ways to create elegance for less, without the savings being apparent to anyone.

Can I promise you that you'll spend one-tenth of the national average? No—but I can help you plan more wedding for what you realistically can afford to spend, giving your bride more than she thought she'd ever have. And that's priceless.

Wedding Budgets by Percentage

I recently surveyed five hundred wedding couples on my Web site www.sharonnaylor.net, and asked them to break down their wedding budgets by percentage. "What percent of your wedding budget are you devoting to your reception menu? To your wedding gown?" for instance. I wanted to show the range of numbers, so that you could see where the average couple is placing the highest amounts of their budget, where they really want to invest for the best outcome. I wasn't a math major in school, so averaging up the numbers isn't on my to-do list here. Instead, I decided to show you the ranges I received, which might help you out with the priorities list I encouraged you to start in the last chapter:

Budget Item	Percentage
Reception (includes menu, drinks, décor, and entertainment)	20–35
Wedding Consultant	15
Wedding Rings	8–15
Flowers	5–20
Photographer and Videographer	5–15
Wedding Gown	3–15
Music	5–10
Bridal Party Apparel	0–3
Rehearsal Dinner	1–5
Tuxedoes	1–4
Invitations	2–4
Gifts to Each Other	2–10
Cake	2–8
Favors	2–4
Bachelor Party	1–2
Attendants' Gifts	1–7
Veil	1–5
Church/Clergy	1–2
Limousine	3–6
Other	5–8

So, as you see, the reception is usually going to take up the bulk of your wedding budget, most likely because it's all about the guests' experience as well. You want the place to look gorgeous, the food to be delicious, the drink to be plentiful and high-quality, and the party to rock. Also up there on the list is the wedding gown, the wedding rings, the flowers, and the photography/videography. Revisit your priorities list now, and see where you feel the primary focus of your budget is going to be. Once you have that nailed down, even without firm and detailed plans on what *exactly* you want for your top-ranking elements, it's time to bring in the parents if they'll have a say in the wedding plans.

"If We Pay, We Have a Say"

Years ago, when brides and grooms married very young, it was almost universal that parents who were paying for the wedding took at the very least an equal hold of the reins and assumed responsibility for many of the wedding plans. Quite often, the very young bride watched helplessly as her mother steamrolled the big day into her own wedding vision (otherwise known as the Wedding Mother Never Had) and Dad grumbled about doling out the cash. The young groom, back then, was out of the loop and just showed up on time for the ceremony, not knowing what anything actually cost. Now things are different.

Today's brides and grooms are waiting to get married, tying the knot at an older and more mature age. They have solid careers, money of their own, they might already own their own homes, have traveled the world, and are very likely to be paying for the wedding themselves. Steamroller Mom is now relegated to showing up on time for the ceremony, not knowing what anything cost, and Dad has far less to grumble about. In fact, the Association of Bridal Consultants (www.bridalassn.com) recently pegged the numbers of fiscal responsibility as follows:

- 53 percent of today's weddings are paid for as a team, with the wedding couple and *both* sets of parents paying for the wedding.
- 27 percent of today's weddings are paid for by the wedding couple themselves.

- 19 percent of today's weddings are paid for by the bride's parents only.
- 1 percent of today's weddings are paid for by someone else (e.g., grandparents, guardians, the groom's parents, maybe even just the bride by herself).

That 53 percent up there might be a welcome sight, since you might feel a bit better about allowing your parents to jump into the cash pool as equal partners with the bride's parents. Or that 27 percent might make you feel proud that you're in a growing percentage of couples who don't need their parents waving the Golden Checkbook at their wedding plans. Whatever your situation, know that the old "rules" are out the window. Weddings are no longer paid for and planned solely by the bride's parents. Freedom reigns in the world of wedding planning, and you're all set to discuss with your bride and your parents exactly how you want to divvy up the wedding costs. Start with the Old World list of who *traditionally* paid for which elements. Not to adhere to those rules, mind you, but just to take a look at how it *used* to be. (Because, trust me, some parent, aunt, or grandparent is going to bring up the issue of "how it's supposed to be" according to the old ways, and you'll want to know what they're talking about):

The Traditional List of Who Pays for What

The Bride's Family Pays For:

- Engagement announcements and photos
- Engagement party
- Bridal consultant
- Ceremony site fees
- Music for the ceremony
- Invitations
- Wedding gown and veil
- Bride's accessories and shoes
- Reception site
- Catering and bar fees
- Flowers for the ceremony and reception sites, bridesmaids' bouquets, and father's boutonnieres
- Entertainment for the cocktail hour and reception
- Photographer
- Videographer
- Reception entertainment
- Limousines and other transportation
- Bridesmaids brunch or luncheon
- Tips

The Bride Pays For:

- Gifts for her bridesmaids and child attendants
- Gift for her groom
- Wardrobe, travel, and lodging for her bridesmaids (optional)
- The wedding programs
- Thank-you notes
- Personal stationery for after the wedding
- Her own wedding day salon visit, including hair, nails, makeup, and so on

The Groom's Family Pays For:

- Officiant's fee
- Marriage license
- Bride's bouquet
- Rehearsal dinner
- Honeymoon (optional)

The Groom Pays For:

- Any of the expenses listed under "Groom's Family Pays For"
- The engagement ring
- Wedding rings (can share this with the bride)
- His own formalwear, shoes, and accessories
- Boutonnieres for himself and the men
- Corsages for the mothers, grandmothers, godmothers
- His attendants' travel and lodging (optional)
- Gifts for his male attendants and the ring bearer

Now, you might find gatherings of parents and stepparents, even grandparents dealing out their claims for individual wedding expenses like so many poker cards, trading the favors for the cake, and even pairing up to assume responsibility for the photographer's bill. Or, you and your bride might wish to pay for everything, but your parents might want to pay for the wedding gown. Fine! That designer gown is $15,000, so let them grab that tab! Or, your parents might stick to the traditional ownership of the rehearsal dinner, which will likely be fine with you. These days, the breakdown of wedding expenses is completely up to you and your co-planners, so take some time, join them all for dinner, and record who wants what from your wedding-planning list.

Be Aware!

Want trouble? Mix together family members and money and potentially watch a violent chemical reaction take place. There's something about money and ego that can take two formerly cordial sets of parents and turn them into pit bulls who are trying to outdo each other financially, judging each other, and fearing that they're being judged because of their financial status. While your sets of parents might not ever plunge to this level, I wanted to bring it up, because you wouldn't be the first couple to stand there dumbfounded watching your parents transform when money is the issue. This can be dramatic, scary, and downright dangerous. Here's how to up the odds of preventing interfamilial dollar envy and fiscal clashes that can drive wedges between your two sides of the family:

- Talk with your bride ahead of time about how best to introduce the "who's paying" issue. She might be able to help you avoid certain wording and phrases that will set her parents off. A little pre-meeting conference is a great idea to get your presentation in top form.

- Speak with respect, but assertively. Let them know that you and your bride have definite wishes and you'd like to invite your parents to join you in planning the wedding. Notice I said, "join you." From minute one, you're establishing boundaries. Very important.

- Never tell your parents what they're going to plan. They need to have at least some say in the matter. Choose which elements of the wedding are up for grabs, and let them enjoy some power as well.

- Show them you're open to their ideas, but not malleable.

- Be ready to explain what things are likely to cost before parents choose to foot the bill for the flowers, the cake, the videographer, and other elements of the wedding. If your parents are like my own father, they might not be up on today's prices and might have a 1970s-era pricetag in mind about those bouquets and centerpieces. Have brochures and Web site printouts available to provide ballpark figures as an introduction to their chosen tasks.

- Be flexible. Let them know they can always change their minds tomorrow.

- Loosen up. Parents can smell fear. Many of us can walk into the boardroom at work and sling figures around with authority, but it's a bit different when you're dealing with Mom and Dad. Even the most self-assured, secure, professional couples tell me that talking dollars with Dad was a knee-shaker. Collect yourself and approach this meeting as just what it is . . . the start to an important negotiation process. And like your clients, Dad will likely respect you more if you're assertive but fair and you know your stuff.
- Plus, every bit of this applies if your parents are *not* involved in the planning, and you're partnering with your bride 100 percent on the financial side of the wedding plans. Good diplomacy and honest money-talk make for a great first step in planning the big day, as well as setting the foundation of your financial partnership after the wedding.

Your Working Budget

Right now, you might not have hard figures on just what each piece of the wedding is going to cost. You might not even have a clear vision of what you want for your wedding. So photocopy this budget worksheet and use it to create an initial, estimated working budget. Start off with the total dollar amount you have to work with, figure in your priorities list, and guesstimate how much you have to spend where. This is important, because when you get to the point of searching for and interviewing every wedding professional from your band to your caterer, your photographer, and the limo company, the first thing they'll want to know is "What's your budget?" You'll need to have numbers on hand before they can help you. So start here on your first pass through the budget, and rough out your numbers.

Before you start, it's a wise move to cross out what you *won't* need money for . . . such as the use of your convertible in place of hiring a limousine for a more casual ride to the party, or the site rental fee if you'll be marrying at a friend's shore house, and so on.

Wedding Budget Worksheet

Item/Service	Who's Paying	Budgeted	Actual
Engagement announcement			
Engagement party			
Ceremony site			
Ceremony décor			
Officiant's fee			
Marriage license			
Blood tests			
Pre-wedding counseling/classes			
Reception site			
Rentals for reception site			
Preparation of reception site (landscaping, cleaning, and so on)			
Additional permits for parking, gathering, and so on			
Wedding gown			
Wedding gown fittings			
Bride's accessories and shoes			
Bridesmaids' wardrobe, shoes, and accessories (if a gift from your bride)			
Bride's manicure, pedicure, and hair			
Groom's clothing			
Groom's accessories			
Financial help with male attendants' wardrobe and accessories (if applicable)			

Item/Service	Who's Paying	Budgeted	Actual
Wedding coordinator			
Invitations			
Postage			
Programs			
Thank-you notes			
Caterer's menu			
Liquor			
Cake			
Flowers			
Reception décor			
Reception entertainment			
Photography			
Videography			
Wedding cameras			
Limousines or classic cars			
Other guest transportation			
Lodging			
Honeymoon suite			
Favors			
Gifts			
Toss-its			
Honeymoon			
Tips			
Taxes			
Other			
Totals			

After a short time during your active wedding expert hunt, you'll switch over to a clean copy of this budget sheet (or one you create on your computer using a financial software program like Quicken) with your harder figures and actual totals. Through the earlier stages of the process, keep your figures fluid so that you can adjust them while still staying within range of your original budget. On page 26, you'll learn some tried-and-true wedding budget rules that will keep you on target, less stressed, and more able to focus on the bigger issues and not just the cash.

Don't Forget the Extras!

As if you're not already stunned by the number of wedding budget categories, I need to remind you about the little extras that can add up along the way. Taxes are a given—they're likely to be included in many of your wedding contracts. But tipping is one of those things that sneaks up on you. It goes without saying that being a great tipper in response to great service is a sign of class, integrity, and respect for others (all traits your bride undoubtedly values in you). So be sure to factor into your budget the tips you're likely to hand out on the wedding day and throughout the planning process. You can carry a wad of cash on you, or you can present envelopes with prearranged amounts in them to each wedding professional you'd like to acknowledge and reward. The usual tipping figures are listed below, but feel free to adjust according to the length and quality of service you receive:

- Site manager: 15–20 percent of total bill for the reception
- Valets: $1 per car
- Waiters: $20–$30 each, depending upon quality of service
- Bartenders: 15 percent of liquor bill
- Limousine drivers: 15–20 percent of transportation bill
- Delivery workers: $10 each if just dropping items off, $20 each if dropping off and setting up
- Tent assemblers and rental agency assemblers: $20 each
- Entertainers: $25–$30 each
- Beauticians: 15 percent–20 percent of beauty salon bill

- Cleanup crew: $20 each
- Baby-sitters or childcare workers: The going rate in your area, plus an extra $20–$30 for the importance of their services, or a gift

Don't forget about any permits you might need for parking, land use, exemption from local noise violations, consumption of alcohol on a beach, cooking on-site, and so on.

Be Aware!

Before you start handing out tips or paying for permits, always triple-check your original hiring contracts to be sure that the gratuity has not already been included. Some companies, such as limousine agencies, automatically add a generous 18 percent tip to your total bill. Sliding a few $20s into the driver's hand after he drops you off can be a waste of money. This is exactly the kind of thing that has tripped up past brides and grooms, who could kick themselves when they realize they have double-tipped. So read the fine print and tip only those whose rewards aren't already billed for.

And be sure to keep some cash on hand on the wedding day for emergencies and the unpredictable. You might have to send home a drunk guest in a cab rather than chance his or her driving home intoxicated. Or you might need to send a groomsman out to the liquor store to get more vodka when the party continues on into the night.

Top 10 Wedding-Budget Rules

1. *Never pay cash: All* wedding charges should be made by credit card for the protection of your investment. (In addition, there are the rewards points, if you have them. Some couples get their honeymoons almost free after charging all of their wedding services.)

2. *Control your budget, but don't be totally controlled by it:* If you stay within 10 percent over or under, you'll be in good shape.

3. *Be organized:* When it comes to your wedding purchases, keep all receipts and deposit records in a binder or envelope. If a vendor argues that you haven't paid, you'll be able to produce the necessary paperwork. This one step can help keep you out of small claims court after the wedding.

4. *Invest only in reliable, proven professionals:* Go through professional organizations to find your experts, ask friends and relatives for referrals to those they hired for their weddings (always the best way!), and never work with a fly-by-night expert or someone who won't give you a detailed, signed contract for his or her work. There are a lot of bad apples out there, so don't wind up on the six o'clock news with a reporter watchdog running down the street after your wedding dress salesperson.

5. *Don't cut too deeply:* This may be a restatement from earlier, but it's truly important to spend and save wisely, never going to either extreme. You'll hate yourself later.

6. *Scrutinize all contracts:* Look for hidden expenses, such as a fee you're asked to pay for a server to cut each slice of wedding cake, and negotiate these fees out of your deal. You can and should make personalized requests like these to all of your wedding experts.

7. *Foster open and honest communication with your bride about the wedding budget:* Don't simmer if you see her getting a little out of control, because you know that's only going to lead to a big fight down the road. Plus, if you're open and noncombative, she is likely to be so as well.

8. *Don't make the money the whole focus:* Some couples get so wrapped up and so stressed out over the dollar factor that they can't enjoy planning their wedding. Yes, spending a fortune on a wedding is always hard, but keep your perspective: This is for a good cause.

9. *Protect others' egos:* If your parents have more expendable income than the bride's family, keep that quiet. Never divulge how much one family

or family member has contributed to your wedding plans, even if you think they're being too generous or too skimpy. Be a gentleman and be discreet.

10. *Don't spend future money:* Yes, your relatives may give you thousands in wedding-gift money, but you should never count on this cash before the fact to cover any shortfall in your wedding budget. Just pretend it's not coming, plan with your present funds, and devote any wedding cash gifts to something for your future . . . like your house or paying off your student loans, your cars, or getting your MBAs.

Money has an undeniable influence over your wedding plans, and it is one of the main causes of stress among marrying couples. It can make your parents squirm; it can make you squirm. But handling it together is good practice for dealing with this issue in your future marriage. Money, along with sex, is likely to be one of the top fighting points forever onward. Use this time and these challenges to prepare *both* of you for the money issues to come . . . working out your finance-handling style now is a big benefit that many couples in the past haven't experienced. While it may sound strange, you're actually lucky to be dealing with this issue now. Use it well, and use your finances well as you plan your ideal wedding day.

3

◇ ◇ ◇

Making It Legal

"Let me see your license, sir."

LEGALLY, the wedding itself means nothing without the documents that put your *marriage* on record. That means your marriage license, proof of marriage eligibility, and a rock-solid prenup if you desire one. Even your chosen house of worship is going to demand to see some proof of your singlehood, such as divorce decrees or a death certificate if one or both of you have been widowed. Without these, even that kindly old priest will turn you away. Yes, we can't let you forget that marriage is a legal proposition, and you must have all of your papers in order before you proceed.

This chapter will help you with reminders to dig through your file cabinet and pull out your birth certificate, divorce papers (if any), and your IDs, and—most important—apply for your marriage license and other important legal papers at the right time.

Getting Your Marriage License

What you may not be aware of right now is that marriage licenses have a shelf life. In some states, you need to actually get married within a month of applying for your license, and in some regions, you can't get married until at least two weeks after applying. Considering that many states (and even individual counties within states!) have different waiting periods, application procedures, and fees for marriage licenses, unwary engaged couples may be confused about the necessary documentation. I receive letter after letter from panicking brides and grooms whose marriage licenses have expired, and thus they need to apply again, paying double and hoping they fit in the window of opportunity. It's one of those mosquito-type hassles . . . a small thing, but a big annoyance.

So where do you start your research about marriage-license rules in the state where you will marry? Start with the county courthouse for the locale where your marriage will take place. Call and ask the registrar to provide you with all the *current* marriage-license requirements. This may sound like a no-brainer, but you'd be surprised how many couples go to the Internet and seek out the details through a bridal Web site. Let me warn you that this is *not* the way to get correct data. Some Web sites contain outdated information; state-wide rules change all the time. So go right to the source and make sure you have the latest available information.

Examples of wedding-license rules and regulations include:

- *You must apply together and in person at the county courthouse or town hall where marriage license applications are issued.*
- *In most states, you must be over the age of 18 to apply for a marriage license without parental consent. If you are under the age of 18, you might need to have a parent accompany you and provide a note of consent for your marriage.*
- *You must have the proper documentation, in original form, in order to apply for a marriage license.*

Where do you apply? Again, that's a state-to-state issue and a question best posed to an official at the county courthouse. Some states allow marrying couples to apply for a license in one county but get married in another county in the same state. Other states require that you apply for your license in the same county where the marriage will take place. This issue greatly affects people who live in one state but will travel back to their home state or out to a favorite resort

Documents You May Need When Applying for Your Marriage License

Different states have different rules, but you might be asked to present any of the following legal documents in order to process your marriage-license application:

- Driver's license
- Birth certificate
- Baptism certificate
- Military identification papers
- Passport or visa
- Divorce decree or valid divorce settlement papers (and know the date and county or location where your divorce was actualized—they're going to want to know!)

Ask for any specific instructions and the documents you'll need.

location to hold their weddings there. For a destination wedding like these, you'll need to check specifically on where you need to apply for your license and perhaps even make special arrangements for both of you to travel to that state for your in-person license application. It takes some extra planning, and maybe some extra mileage, but it must be done.

What to Watch For

Watch that calendar closely, because most marriage licenses are only valid for a period of 60 to 90 days. Add to that timing challenge the fact that some states require 24- to 48-hour waiting periods between issuing the marriage license and the date of your wedding. If you don't have your valid time well mapped, you may have a big problem.

What About Blood Tests?

Before you tie the knot, the state's going to want some blood. And perhaps a few other things. It's true that some states are now dropping the blood test requirement, choosing not to test engaged couples for sexually transmitted diseases as they have in the past. But some states still require tests for HIV, syphilis, and a range of other conditions before they'll grant you the all's clear for marriage. At the time of this writing, Indiana and Montana were two states that required only the *bride* to get a blood test, so you can see how subjective individual states can be about their blood test rules. Check with your county courthouse to find out which medical tests are required.

The Care and Handling of Your License

Whatever you do, don't lose that paper! Stick it to the fridge, put it in a safe, find a secure place for it. On your wedding day, your officiant and witnesses are going to need to sign that paper to make your marriage a legal entity. After the wedding, that's the form you and your bride will use to submit your new marital status to your insurance companies, workplace, the IRS, Social Security, and all other important agencies. (For more on marital status and name change, see page 39.) This license is your ticket to official coupledom, so consider it golden.

Prenuptial Agreements

Speaking of golden, your own assets might be golden to you—as your fiancée's may be golden to her—and you'll be right in line with current trends if you're thinking about formulating a prenuptial agreement. I can hear legions of brides-to-be screaming right now about how prenups are an insult, that they take the romance out of marriage, and that they signal a stunning lack of confidence that this marriage is going to last. "How can I feel like you love me if you're worried about protecting your IRA/car/CDs/house?" is the refrain. True, bringing up the whole prenup issue can be a powder keg, but more and more couples today find themselves in complete agreement on the topic.

Think about it . . . today's marrying couple is older, more financially secure, might own their own home(s), have some significant assets and life experience before they settle down in a permanent partnership. With all of that individual gain built up, who would want to see a judge divvy up your loot in the event of the worst? We live in a more litigious society than ever, but we're also a smarter society when it comes to protecting our own asses . . . I mean, assets. So both partners might be fine with the whole prenup thing.

You Might Want a Prenuptial Agreement If . . .

- You or your spouse have significant assets of your own before marriage
- You or your spouse have children from a previous relationship (This is the #1 reason for prenups among couples today—parents want to make sure the kids' inheritance will go to them and not automatically to a spouse. In the event of your death, your kids shouldn't have the extra trauma of going into probate.)
- You or your spouse owns a business, or a share in a business
- You or your spouse comes into the marriage carrying some debt, or you have concerns with your partner's propensity for gathering debt
- There are other issues of significant importance to you

When you decide to look into the mechanics of your own potential prenuptial agreements, a good lawyer can lead you through your particular requests and requirements. Most prenups provide for a claim on individual assets, a solid plan for financial support in the event of a split, and even plans for child custody of kids you don't have yet. While celebrities often make us laugh with their seemingly ridiculous prenup terms ("You cheated on me? That's one million bucks, buddy. And you *lied* about it? That's five million more. Make the cashier's check out to . . ."), you should know that the courts are quite savvy about perceived manipulative language in a prenup. Outrageous requests and claims are not likely to hold up in court—not that you'd stick it to your fiancée at this point and hope she doesn't notice you've asked her to sign all of her future wages over to you if she gains more than twenty pounds during your marriage!

What to Watch For

Judges watch for signs of forced compliance, meaning the prenup was signed by your shaking and frazzled bride five minutes before the Wedding March started playing on the wedding day. If a judge smells coercion, your prenup gets thrown out. This is part of the reason that more and more attorneys are *videotaping* the final discussions and signing of premarital agreements, providing proof that both partners were fully aware of the terms they agreed to.

Looking into prenuptial agreements might be a wise move for both of you, and more of an investment in your future than a shameless announcement of doubt about your partnership. Many couples I spoke to said that while they can understand the uproar about how unromantic and pessimistic a prenup can seem right before you're about to marry, they found theirs to bring about greater peace of mind, knowing that whatever the future might bring, they weren't going to wind up being stripped of their hard-earned assets (and future children!) by an unfeeling court. It depends which school of thought you subscribe to, and how you and your fiancée look at this topic. It may not even be an issue for you.

Again, a rock-solid lawyer can lead you through the process if you're interested in exploring the world of prenuptial agreements, looking through your financial paperwork, asking the right questions, and building a customized legal agreement for the two of you. While there are downloadable forms out there on the Internet, as well as packaged do-it-yourself legal software, I strongly advise you to hire an attorney. Such an important document should really be handled by a pro who knows more about the ins and outs of prenups than you might glean from a template program.

On the Web

To find an attorney who specializes in family or marital law and the creation of prenuptial agreements, go to www.abanet.org, the Web site for the American Bar Association. There you can conduct a search of bar-approved attorneys in your area. Or find an attorney on your own; maybe a friend has been happy with similar services from his lawyer. Some terms to check out are *premarital agreements*, *antenuptial agreements*, and *prenuptial agreements*—all mean the same thing. Also, keep in mind that both you and your fiancée should hire separate lawyers for this process, as one lawyer should not represent both of you.

One last note on premarital agreements. It's not too late if you don't have one signed and sealed before your wedding day. Now you can create protective postmarital or postnuptial agreement between the two of you at any time during your marriage. The procedure is similar—you will both want to consult your own attorney.

Wedding Insurance

If you say the words "protected and secure" to your bride right now, she's not going to think prenuptial agreements right away. To her, "protected and secure" might more readily apply to all the plans for the wedding day itself. And that's where wedding insurance comes in.

We've all heard horror stories about the weddings where a downpour collapsed the tent, a hurricane blew into town and kept all of the guests from being able to get there, the cake fell to the ground, and the photographer didn't show up. We've seen the funniest home videos on television where various wedding catastrophes might make us giggle and grab for another Doritos chip, but you know the drenched bride with the smashed cake in *that* wedding was not in a snacking mood. More like a *smacking* mood—when her groom lost the wedding rings or her dress fell apart at the seams due to shoddy alterations. And we've all seen television court show episode where some sad-faced wedding couple attempts to sue their caterer/photographer/florist/cake baker/hair stylist for frighteningly bad service on the wedding day . . . and they have the pictures to prove it!

Wedding-based lawsuits keep small claims courts hopping, and it's no wonder when you take into account the sheer expense of weddings, the importance of all the little and big details, and the dependence you may have on all the wedding professionals who have promised you their best work. And then there's the weather. Hurricanes, snowstorms, ice storms, lightning, weather-related travel hassles—all can wreak havoc on the best-laid wedding plans.

When you're planning a day this important, you'll want to protect all of your investments, so that you'll get some of that money back if what can go wrong does go wrong. Sure, it might not make up for the loss of the wedding dream to get a refund in the mail, but it's better to get that check than not get it.

There is a big boom in wedding insurance policies these days, and it's a good idea for you to check them out. Remember, some people will sue if their coffee is too hot or if they forgot to take the toothpick out of a finger sandwich before inhaling it. Wedding professionals carry huge insurance policies to protect against unforeseen dilemmas, to protect their livelihoods, and so might you wish to protect your wedding day with your own policy.

Wedding insurance is available in many different plans and at many different expense levels. Premiums vary according to your region and the size of the wedding you have in mind, and they can partially or fully protect you against a handful of the most common wedding disasters, like the following:

- The wedding officiant not showing up
- Either you or your groom suffering injury or illness to the point of not being able to make it to the wedding
- The photographer losing the negatives of your wedding photos
- Your caterer going out of business the day before the wedding
- The church or reception hall suddenly closed and off-limits for your wedding
- Extremely bad weather that prevents the guests from reaching the wedding or causes the event to be called off altogether (This means a tornado destroying your reception hall, not a heavy rain preventing you from having your pictures taken outside!)

- Someone walking into the reception and stealing all of the wedding gifts or wedding money envelopes
- Bad weather preventing you, your guests, or an important vendor from being able to make it to the wedding
- You or your fiancée being called up for active military duty, and in some cases in the event of a last-minute corporate move

For extra fees, you might be able to cover damage to your wedding gifts, rented items, and wedding wardrobes, with the exclusion of your jewelry.

In the Event of Bodily Harm . . .

You can also purchase a wedding personal liability plan that pays up to $500,000 in the case of property damage or bodily harm to a guest during the course of your insured wedding. That would cover the hot coffee and that hidden toothpick very nicely, along with the following:

- Injury to a guest
- Injury to a member of the site's staff
- Property damage, such as a thrown bouquet knocking down and shattering part of the ballroom chandelier (it happens *so* often)
- Property damage caused by a vendor, such as when those bananas flambée are dramatically lit and the drapes catch fire
- Property damage, such as a glass of red wine spilled on a white rug or couch or a vase knocked from its pedestal
- Drunk driving incidents, such as an inebriated guest smashing into another parked car while attempting to leave your event (This one alone is worth the cost of insurance. At one recent wedding, a guest leaving the event was killed in a drunk-driving accident after refusing to hand over his keys. The guest's widow sued the bride and groom as hosts of the event where the alcohol was served. Don't put yourself in jeopardy this way. Consider coverage.)

Add in wedding medical coverage, and you might get up to $1,000 total for guests' claims.

Not everything is covered by wedding or special event insurance policies, though. Your individual plan might have some interesting limitations. One popular plan does *not* cover the best man losing the wedding rings, the bride's dress falling apart, or one of you getting cold feet and backing out of the wedding altogether. (Actually, most wedding insurance plans don't cover "cold feet" cancellations, so you're on your own with that one.)

Obviously, there's an "It's something we couldn't prevent" issue that determines what's covered and what's not covered by wedding insurance policies. Regardless of the legalities, couples are still flocking to Web sites like WedSafe (www.wedsafe.com) and Fireman's Fund Wedsurance (800-ENGAGED [364-2433]), as well as their own insurance handlers to check out the offerings, investigate policy premiums and plans, and read what other couples have to say about insurance saving the big day. An interesting example is one in which a solid insurance plan will pay to have all of your main wedding guests flown back in on a set day to re-create the most picture-worthy scenes from your ceremony and reception in the event that your day-of photographs do not come out. New photos are then taken so that you don't spend forever without any record of your day. That's the kind of rescue wedding insurance can deliver.

And what does all this protection cost you? Not much. For a basic plan that covers your deposits, rings, photos, video, and wedding day outfits, you can expect to pay between $150 and $300. For general liability insurance (always a good idea these days), you might spend between $150 and $250. Not bad for what could be a half-million to a million-dollar policy! For the same price as wedding favors, you could be saving yourselves from a major lawsuit or two.

Be sure to apply for wedding insurance as soon as possible. Some companies will not cover your event if you apply less than two or three weeks before your wedding date, so the sooner you act, the better.

You can get any kind of policy or policies to suit your wedding. There's special event insurance, personal liability insurance, and special riders to your homeowner's insurance policy to cover anything that might happen to any of your guests or houseguests throughout the wedding weekend. If you're having an at-home or outdoor wedding, or a big-budget wedding, you'd be wise to at least talk with an insurance provider about the kinds of coverage that might be a smart buy. Talk to your own insurance agent, look into wedding and special event coverage, and get the numbers that will affect your wedding budget. See where you need to cover yourself and where your wedding professionals have covered themselves (and never hire a wedding professional who is not insured!). You might find, once again, that the peace of mind in being covered against the unknown is worth every penny.

Is She Taking Your Name?

Today's bride has a choice to make. After the wedding, she might take the last name of her groom, keep her own last name, or hyphenate the two. Even grooms are getting in on the name-change game, sometimes opting to hyphenate *their* names too. And there are some trailblazing couples out there who adopt the *bride's* last name for both of them, or even choose an entirely new alternative last name for themselves.

If surnames are changing, it's time to look into the legalities and procedures for getting that changed name on record everywhere it matters. Here is where you can help your bride out, if she is planning on making the change:

Once the marriage license is signed after the ceremony, the bride (and perhaps you) will need to complete all of the notifications about change of name and marital status on every identification and account you have. You'll start with that completed and registered license (which you will either take with you after the wedding, or have mailed to you after registry, depending on your state's rules) and go first to Social Security. You'll need a corrected Social Security card for many of your future name alterations.

On the Web

To start the process of changing a name at Social Security, go to the Web site at www.ssa.gov or www.socialsecurity.gov and download the form for a new, updated card. Or call 800-772-1213 to have the forms sent to you. Then you can either hand in your old card in person (along with your official marriage license and identification such as a driver's license) or mail it in for exchange.

Next to be notified of your name-change should be:

- Work: Your name needs to be changed on record so that your pay, health insurance, 401(k), and work-related access cards can be updated.
- The bank: They'll need your new ID to change your accounts and issue new documentation to match your name on all of your investment plans and MAC accounts, stock and bond accounts, and IRAs.
- The IRS
- Department of Motor Vehicles: Your car registration and driver's license need to be changed.
- Post office
- Phone voice mail services
- Internet services
- Credit card companies
- Loan agencies
- Insurance companies
- Car leasing center
- Utility companies
- Doctors' offices
- Consumer cards, such as video rental, department store member shopper's services, club cards
- Gym membership
- Passport
- Voter registration
- Alumni clubs
- Magazine subscriptions
- Any other important agencies and resources

> **On the Web**
>
> A great resource is www.weddingchannel.com's complete state-by-state name-change guide, which provides details on name-change procedures, time limits, fees, and where to go to make the switch.

A Timesaver Note for Your Bride: Along the way, friends and family can be notified of the name change through a quick e-mail or postcard blitz informing everyone of your new identity. What matters most is that you're on record as *you* across the board, legally, everywhere that matters.

Sign by the X

I'm sure you've dealt with contracts before, so I'll just reiterate that *all* quality wedding vendors should provide you with a highly detailed contract outlining their terms of service. This is your legal agreement, so you need to take the time to read the fine print, speak up to request additions, changes, and—most important—the writing-down of all verbal agreements between the vendor and yourselves. That means itemized lists of what you've chosen for your floral order and bar menu, times of delivery, and special changes to their packages.

Take the contract home with you if you need additional time to read it before signing, and work only with vendors who are agreeable about changes you wish to make to their contracts. There's a lot in that fine print that you'll be bound to, so do the right thing and take the time to know what you're signing. Too many couples, overwhelmed with the sheer mass of wedding planning details, do not take the time to sit back and read through the documents. I hope you won't make this mistake.

You can ask many wedding professionals for a "time is of the essence" clause, which states that the vendor is legally bound by contract to deliver the flowers, cake, food, and so on by a stated time of day or else they're in breach of contract. This may seem a little bit too detailed, but trust me . . . wedding setup needs to be a finely tuned machine, with everything in place right as it's needed. Wedding professionals can and should be bound to their promises of timely delivery, or else your bride might walk down the aisle without her bouquet. You might not have thought about this detail, but make sure that phrase "time is of the essence" is somewhere in all your contracts in which on-time provision is key.

Another high-priority subject in any contract is the cancellation and refund policy. Be sure you know the terms if you should for any reason wish to cancel with this pro and go with another. See if you're locking into a no-refund deal.

Keep all your signed contracts organized and in a safe place, in case you need to refer to them after the wedding.

4

◇ ◇ ◇

Start Spreading the News

IN THE TIME IT TAKES YOU to blink twice, your fiancée, her mother, and your mother have probably already notified about half of their friends and family of your impending wedding. Your fiancée is showing off her ring to anyone who can see, Mom's already on her way to the bookstore to pick up an armload of bridal magazines and books, and the rollercoaster ride is beginning to pick up speed.

This is the fun stuff, where you get to spread the good news and celebrate with everyone who's close to you. Right off the bat, you may find yourselves as the guests of honor at an engagement party (or two or three) thrown by parents, friends, or colleagues. Oh, yes, the parties start right away, so make sure you join your fiancée in registering for your most wished-for wedding gifts right away, so that guests can get you the great stuff you want.

Your Engagement Announcement

Couples are taking a few weeks before they put their official engagement announcement in the town newspapers where both they and their parents live . . . if they even place an announcement at all. Some couples choose instead to go the Internet route with the creation of a wedding Web site (more on that later in this chapter) where the wording is not so formulaic. If you do wish to go the traditional

What's on Your Registry Wish List?

Marrying couples register for gifts at two or three different stores these days, and they're not just signing up for fine china, crystal, linens, and a blender. Now that couples are marrying later, they might already have all the kitchen appliances and towels they need. And make no mistake, grooms are enthusiastically on board for this non-shopping trek, aiming the laser guns at price tags and recording the model numbers of such things as luggage, tool sets, home entertainment systems, mountain bikes, artwork, yard furniture, and even kayaks. Forget that bagel-cutter or the breadmaker. Now you can register at Home Depot, sporting supply stores, even gourmet wine and liquor stores to get your wine cellar started and your humidor filled. At Bridal Home Registry (www.thebridalhomeregistry.com), you can create a registry where guests can contribute toward your own near-future home purchase. The world of bridal registries has opened up to the men, so see what kinds of things you and your future wife want in your future home, and sign right up.

route with an engagement announcement in the paper (or if your parents have taken over this task, which is often the case), you will contact the newspaper, request a form for engagement announcements, or dictate your vitals to the editor. Your names, place of residence, parents' names and their places of residence, your jobs, the month of your wedding . . . all get written up in a brief and tidy announcement of your big news. You might or might not include a formal or informal portrait of the two of you to include in your announcement.

The "Honey, we made the papers!" moment can be exciting when you see yourselves in print and your e-mail and phone does double-volume when friends and acquaintances send their congrats.

Your Wedding Web Site

Here is one wedding task in which you might be only too happy to get involved: setting up a personalized, interactive wedding Web site that details everything about your upcoming wedding for all your friends and family to see. The explosion in bridal Web site popularity now points to the fact that we live in a global society where our circle of loved ones live all over the country and perhaps the world. And what better way to share information globally (and at lightning speed) than through the Internet? Once you set up your Web site, everyone from your hometown friends to your clients in Brazil and Australia, your grandmother in Maine, and your brother in Memphis, just has to log on to your site to find out everything, including directions to the reception location, where you're registered (plus a link to take them right to your list), and the plans for the entire wedding weekend. Your buddies will know to bring their golf clubs, and the ladies will know to pack their little black dresses for a pre-planned night on the town.

Disseminating vital information to your guests is perhaps *the* primary advantage of creating a wedding Web site—which can list directions, phone numbers to the hotel, scheduling for bridal party fittings, and other details that you would otherwise have to make a few dozen phone calls to inform people about. It's a time-saver, an efficient tool for organizing everyone involved with your wedding, from your best man to your guests. With many of us living at such great distances, this site is the best way to get the legwork done in an instant . . . and share the fun stuff as well.

What I love about wedding Web sites is that guests who visit them can get a lot more than just directions to the reception hall, links to the hotel and registry, and other purely useful things. These sites are fun, highly personalized accounts that can get guests excited about the big event way before the actual day. Some examples of hot wedding Web site features that you might choose to use on yours are:

- Photo galleries of you and your bride, including pictures from the night of your engagement, vacations you've taken together, and even baby or childhood pictures of both of you for the "aren't they cute?" factor
- Video streamed "welcome to our site" messages from you to the site visitor, or even footage of you popping the question (if you got that on film)
- Pictures and bios of your bridal party (so they can scope out who they'll hit on at your wedding)
- Message boards guests can use to share information and questions with you and with other guests

- Quizzes for guests to take about the two of you, including such questions as how the two of you met or where you took her on your first date
- Surveys and polls for guests to take, such as "You get a vote in what our first-dance song should be," along with a list of song titles
- A running day-by-day or hour-by-hour countdown to your wedding day
- Photo-shopped graphics, jokes, comic strips, and other laugh-worthy features you can add to a lighthearted page
- Background music of your choice, from classical to party music to the Wedding March

These features can be great fun for your guests, and they can follow your online journal to see how the planning is coming along. With regular updates of written and picture areas, even your guests from across the globe can be a part of your wedding. For instance, a visit to your site might provide a distant relative's or friend's first look at your bride.

Expert Input

Todd Meikle, together with his wife Krista, is the founder and president of www. wedstudio.com, a hot new site that helps you to build your own wedding Web site using their custom program. When I spoke with Todd, he said that grooms are jumping at the chance to log on: "In the past, the grooms pretty much just stayed out of the way while the bride and her mother did all the wedding planning. Now, with this kind of fun, tech Web site to mess around with, [it's giving] grooms more of an incentive to get involved. What's happening is that the bride is usually writing up the wording for their About Us sections, bios of the bridal party, and other areas, and the grooms are downloading those files as well as all the pictures they'll have on the site. It's a great way for grooms to contribute with their abilities and tech knowledge, even if they're not too techno, and the bride loves that they're working together on something that's important to the big day."

For a look at what you can create as your own wedding Web site, visit the Wed Studio site.

Wedding Announcements

You can also send out wedding announcements to people who aren't going to be on your wedding guest list as a way to share your good news with them. This can be done after the wedding, just to let all your far-flung friends and acquaintances know that you got hitched. Some couples worry that sending out announcements is a great way to offend people ("Hey, why wasn't I invited?!"), but just relax. An announcement is a nice way of letting people know, without obligating them to get you a present. It's just good form, after the fact. If it will make you feel better, send out announcements with any leftover favors from the wedding, or with something sweet like a candy bar or a picture from your day.

5

◇ ◇ ◇

Choosing Your Men

NAMING BRIDAL PARTY ATTENDANTS is probably going to be a *much* bigger deal to your bride than to you. While she's stressing over which five of her closest friends she'll invite to be her bridesmaids, you might name your groomsmen in five seconds flat. Men don't get all wrapped up in the whole "If I don't invite him into the circle, he'll get offended" thing. You name your brothers, your best buddies, and even the bride's brothers if you're close to them. Case closed. Time for lunch.

But while this may not be a highly emotional or complex choice for you, it is an important one in terms of function. The men you choose need to be reliable, available to attend the prewedding and wedding weekend events, and they need to be your closest male cohorts. But even more important, these are the guys who are going to plan your bachelor party, so choose well.

Bridal Party Criteria

The men you choose to stand up for you as your side of the bridal party need to be not only your closest buddies and family members, they need to possess certain qualities that make them fit for the *roles* they'll play during the wedding process in its entirety. Being named a groomsman or best man is not just a title, it's a job.

Not a big job, but it's a job. And you'll need to choose men who can pull off their responsibilities and make a good showing for you on the wedding day. So that slacker friend of yours who is likely to show up late, unshaven, and hung over for the ceremony might not be your best bet. These guys need to be presentable, or you're going to hear it from your bride. The qualities you're looking for in a male attendant are reliability, integrity, good social skills, and a history of being there for you. You know these guys aren't going to fail you. And you wouldn't want anyone else by your side as you take this important leap.

Another set of factors is the ability to perform the role. Is the guy going to be able to attend the wedding? Distance might be a factor in some cases, but in most cases, plane rides are not going to stop your closest buddies and brothers from getting to your wedding in time. I've heard stories of guys who took the red-eye out from Seattle to make it to the wedding the next morning. And I have also heard many stories of groomsmen and best men who drove cross-country in the weeks after September 11 to get to a wedding when most of the other guests canceled. It's a sign of your guys' loyalty to you that they'd go to such great lengths to be there. And you know which friends would drive through a hurricane to get there for the two of you.

The next factor: money. Is your guy hurting for cash, or will he be able to afford the tux rental? You can foot the bill for him if money is a factor. But it is something to keep in mind. Several grooms have written to me to complain about groomsmen who claim poverty when it comes to the wedding, but then take weekend trips to Cancun with their girlfriends. You can't teach your friends to be fiscally responsible, but I wouldn't want you to be stuck with a named groomsman and then have to consider the diplomatic and social repercussions of firing him from the lineup. If you fear in the least that one of your main men isn't going to pull his weight, leave him off your list. The chosen few need to be able to step up and take care of business. That should be your main priority in selecting them.

What About Women?

One of the most interesting trends in modern bridal parties is *female* attendants on the groom's side. If you are among the adventurous guys to select a woman

Be Aware!

Don't get shoved into naming someone to your bridal party. I know a recently married couple who allowed themselves to be bossed into naming a groomsman because he was the best friend of one of the other groomsmen, part of their close social circle, and he rounded out the bridal party to make it a matching number of men and women. But the couple never saw this guy again. So there he is in their wedding video and pictures, and they don't even like him. He was a buffoon then, and he's a buffoon now. Someday this couple will have to explain to their kids who that guy on the end of the line in their wedding pictures was. Skip the pity invites and the social-push invites and choose only those men you're sure you'll know in ten years.

attendant, she'll be called your groomswoman or a groom's attendant, and she'll stand with your men. Say you have a close female friend from childhood, and you really want her to be a part of your inner circle. The bride wouldn't necessarily choose her to be a part of the bridesmaids' lineup, since she already has too many sisters, friends, cousins, colleagues, and sorority sisters to consider. That "men only" rule for your attendants' list has been thrown out the window, and now you can invite this friend to stand up for you. Just as the bride can ask her closest male friend to be a part of her lineup. . . . minus the lavender dress to match the bridesmaids'. Her attendant wears a tuxedo like yours, and your female attendant has her choice of wearing a dress like that of the bridesmaids, or a great black dress to match your black tuxes. (In fact, she might be the luckiest woman in the bridal party to be able to opt out of wearing those blush pink gowns with the scarf and matching dyed shoes!)

Whatever the fashion, your freedom to choose a female attendant is in style. So don't close the door on your best gal friend. She can have a place next to you as well.

Two Best Men?

Can't choose between your brother and your best friend from childhood for the ultimate role of best man? Perhaps you really want your best friend, but your family will flip if you don't name your brother. Happens all the time. So just give them both the title and be done with it. There's no rule that says you can have only one best man. These days, you'll find grooms with two best men, their father as their best man, and even a female counterpart called the best lady. Grooms with children might have their sons as best men and daughters as best girls. The sky is not even a limit when it comes to creative title bestowing, so you shouldn't feel limited when you're making your choice.

Or, forget your brother and just choose your best friend. He'll get over it.

Question About Groomsmen

My fiancée has two brothers whom I know only casually from a few family parties. They live far away and will attend the wedding. But should I invite them to be my groomsmen as well? I have enough guy friends and brothers of my own to fill the slots.

The answer: It's up to you and your bride. Talk with her and see how she feels about it, and if she's planning on asking her brothers' wives or girlfriends/fiancées to be a part of her bridesmaids' list. It's always a good move family-wise to include the brothers. Leaving them out could be a major faux pas with her parents. So consider the choice and the aftermath, and make your move.

Uneven Numbers?

So you have six male attendants on your list, and your bride has seven bridesmaids. Do you scrounge up another guy to even out the numbers? Encourage her to eliminate a cousin? Nope. You *can* have an uneven number of men and maids in the bridal party. The only place where it's evident is at the ceremony, and you'd simply have one groomsman escort two of the ladies back down the aisle during the recessional. Simple as that.

Choosing Your Best Man

Your best man is an honored man of the hour. You've chosen him for his years of support, closeness, and reliability. But you've also chosen him to perform some extra duties the other men won't have. It might be helping you out with your tasks in the wedding planning, providing support to you in those hours when your fiancée is driving you nuts, your future father-in-law is grilling you about your career plans, and your mother is freaking out about the color of the dress the bride wants her to wear. Your best man may be the guy who gets you out of there for a few beers or a day trip to a minor league baseball game. He's the guy who's going to be your support and rescuer from the world of the wedding and what it does to everyone involved in planning it.

Put his number on your speed dial, if you haven't already, because you will need his sense of humor from now until well after you've begun to settle into married life.

I asked dozens of grooms what their best men did for them and for the wedding plans, what the brides and grooms appreciated the most about his contributions. Here are some of the things they had to say:

* *"He was so reliable. He organized the groomsmen for their tuxedo ordering, reminded them to send in their size cards, hounded those who hadn't paid, and made sure all the guys showed up on time to pick up their tuxes. Then he returned the tuxes by the deadline so we didn't incur extra charges."*

* *"He was a great motivator. He can get others to do things without knowing they've just been told what to do."*

* *"He just cracked us up when we needed it most. Especially during the ceremony when the unity candles wouldn't light. He just pretended to be blowing them out, and everyone lightened up. Even my bride started laughing, when I thought she was more likely to cry about that."*

When you're choosing your best man, you want to be sure he's good in social situations, because he becomes a sort of host at the wedding. He'll need to mingle, introduce guests if necessary, and then there's his big moment at the mike: the best man's toast. He's the guy who makes the first big speech of the reception and the opener to the entire celebration. He sets the tone for the party, so he needs to be a decent public speaker.

The best best man's toasts are short, funny, and sentimental. He'll say something about when he first met the bride, and he'll know enough not to say anything offensive or off-color about her or about you. He likes your bride, and he'll tell the whole room that the two of you are a perfect match. And he'll be mostly sober while doing it. His great speech can lead off your great reception.

Your Main Men: What They Need to Do

Here is the list of responsibilities all of your men will have before and during your wedding day:

- Attend all prewedding parties such as engagement parties and any co-ed showers thrown for you and your bride
- Get measured for tuxedo rental
- Shop for socks, shoes, and accessories
- Pick up wedding day wardrobe at appointed time
- Attend all planned wedding weekend activities such as softball tournament or round of golf
- Help transport guests to their hotels (optional)
- Plan and attend bachelor party
- Attend wedding rehearsal and learn requirements and special instructions
- Attend rehearsal dinner
- Take groom out on morning of the wedding for breakfast, to play golf, and so on (optional)
- Arrive on time on the wedding day
- Escort guests to their seats at the ceremony (ushers and groomsmen do this)
- Stand on groom's line during the ceremony (all male attendants)
- Party at the reception

The Little Guys

If your bridal party will include ring bearers, you'll need to decide who these darling little guys will be and ask their parents for permission to have them act as part of your event. Parents know best what their kids' temperaments are, whether they're old enough and mature enough to be given such roles during a wedding. Plus, parents will be the ones assuming the responsibility for getting the kids' outfits and accessories for the big day, perhaps paying for travel and lodging as well, so coordinating with the parents is a must.

Guys Who Don't Make the Cut

If you're such a popular and much-loved guy that you can't possibly fit all of your buddies into your bridal party, then you might wish to find other high-profile positions of honor for your close guy friends to fill. While these might not be usher or groomsmen roles, they do hold a place of importance. Such as . . .

- Reading a passage during the ceremony
- Participating in religious rituals during the ceremony, such as bringing the wine to the altar
- Participating in cultural rituals during the ceremony, such as presenting the crown of olive leaves if your ceremony includes that, or placing the broom for you to jump over after you're married
- Performing a musical number at the ceremony if his gift is music. He might sing or play piano if he's trained and talented enough.
- Releasing the doves after the ceremony
- Acting as emcee during the reception, leading the party and introducing the two of you into the room
- Proposing or taking part in a toast to the two of you
- Proposing a toast during the reception
- Reading well-wisher e-mails or letters from guests who couldn't attend during the reception
- Introducing any special performances during the ceremony, such as a singer you've hired to serenade your bride
- Performing a song at the reception
- Introducing a specially-edited video montage of you and your bride, for playing during the reception or cocktail hour (especially if *he* was the video editor). Note: Such personalized video airings during receptions are all the rage—guests love seeing childhood videos of you two as kids, plus special times during your courtship and the preparations for the wedding. . . .

What matters most is that you include your special friends *somehow*, in roles that they're comfortable with. Don't forget: Some guys might want to be in your wedding party, but they might not be able to. For whatever reason, they have wisely and self-knowingly informed you that they just can't fulfill all the roles necessary to be a part of your wedding, so they might have had to turn down your invitation. If this happens due to how far away they live, special family circumstances, or tight finances, then it's best to find this good man another role that fits within his capabilities.

As for the bachelor party. . . . We'll get to that later in the book.

6

◇ ◇ ◇

Working with the Bride
(and Everyone Else, Too)

When it comes to working with your bride on anything having to do with the wedding, here is the only thing you need to know. . . .

The correct answer is "*Yes, dear.*"

I could have ended this entire chapter right there, since brevity is best and that one answer cuts right to the chase, but I'll go on to discuss the intricacies of dealing with *what happens* to your bride during the duration of the wedding planning. Because she's very likely to take on an entirely different personality. They have all kinds of names for what happens to a mild-mannered, even-keeled, and very pulled-together bride when the wedding plans start spewing and the unbelievable level of stress starts getting to her: *Bridezilla* being the most commonly tossed-around title these days. We in the wedding industry have seen grooms sit there stunned while their lovely brides go all red in the face and veins start throbbing in their necks and foreheads while they shriek about incorrect placement of postage stamps on envelopes. One last straw, and your bride could lose it too.

You've undoubtedly seen her at her worst. When she's sick and cranky, angry as hell at some unjustifiable power play at the office, or when she's just in a bitchy mood for no particular reason. You loved her even in her worst moods. But there's very little preparation for what you might see when your own bride turns into a banshee and is very much *not* the picture of the radiant bride-to-be. In short, things can get ugly.

Of course, not all brides blow their tops to this degree, but I assure you . . . unless the two of you are running off to Vegas in the middle of the night with no more wedding planning than packing a suitcase and leaving a voice mail for your parents, there *is* going to be at least one wedding-related meltdown somewhere along the road. And you could be right in the middle of it.

So for the sake of present and future harmony with your bride, I'm going to help you out with a few basic rules for keeping a firm grip on your bride's hand even when the wedding plans turn her into a scary version of herself. If you're partnering with her on the plans, you'll need the do's and don'ts that come down in legend from grooms who have gone before you. And I'll also give you the one phrase you should *never* say if you want to keep your face intact.

Later on in this chapter, you'll also learn a few pointers about working with others during the planning process, because parents and future in-laws (even grandparents!) can lose their minds over the wedding and show you a whole new side of themselves as well. As the stable, sturdy, dependable groom and all-around rock for the bride, you'll need some deflection tips for when others attack as well.

What's Making Her So Crazy?

Most men just shrug and say "What's the big deal?" when their bride is in tears over what her mother is planning to wear to the wedding. Guys just don't get it when brides lose their cool over something that seems so small and insignificant. But I promise you that whatever your bride is sobbing over is just the tip of the iceberg. When we lose it over something trivial, the bigger picture and the rest of the iceberg underneath the surface is frustration. A lot of built-up frustration. A *lot*.

Your bride might have started off the wedding plans full of joy and anticipation. She might have been very flexible and happily working with her parents and your parents all along the way. Things seemed just fine. But underneath, she might have been storing up one grain of sand after another on some invisible scale—one insensitive comment from her mother, one subtle dig from her father, a few off-color remarks from a jealous bridesmaid, half a dozen pushy suggestions from the wedding coordinator. And like that proverbial scale, it might just take one little, tiny thing to tip the scale over to the other side. You never saw it coming, but she's felt it coming for a long time, even though she smiled the whole way through.

Different brides have different tolerance points for swallowed stress, and they also have different ways of processing their frustrations. Your bride might be basket-case material soon, or she might hold her sense of humor all the way through and *never* freak out over anything. Which example your bride is going to resemble is up to her for the most part, but you also hold a big-time key to her emotional well-being. You might be able to prevent Bridal Meltdown.

Here's what most of the brides I deal with have to say about what makes them crazy during the months before the wedding:

- *"Everyone has an opinion—even over the smallest things. And over time, my patience has worn thin. Can't everyone just shut up about the napkins, the centerpieces, the favors? When did this get to be any of their business?"*

- *"All my mother has to do is give me 'the look' and I turn into an eight-year-old. I don't know how she manages to push my buttons like that. But she's driving me crazy, and then I'm mad at myself that I reacted like such a child. I'm smarter than that."*

- *"If I hear one more 'What will people think?' from his mother, I'm going to scream."*

- *"I can never get my wedding coordinator on the phone, and when I do, it's usually her telling me that we can't get some kind of flower or food or favor that I asked for. But she's happy to recommend things she'd* like *to see at my wedding. Why can't she just try a little harder?"*

If these quotes sound whiny, it's because they are. These brides were well into the wedding-planning process, and several of them were already operating at about half their maturity level. We regress when we're exhausted. And for many, working with opinionated mothers-in-law, guilt-tripping parents, disagreeable bridesmaids, and jealous sisters is exhausting. Add in the frustration of dealing with wedding experts who never took the course called The Customer Is Always Right, and you're looking at a major meltdown pretty soon.

Brides get pushed and pulled in many directions, owing to their wishes to have everything exactly as they want it versus their families wanting everything the way *they* want it. It's a classic power struggle, and there are hundreds of books on the difference between how men and women handle power struggles, and relationships, and the difference between handling and controlling situations. Your bride might be having a problem with handling all those wedding-related situations. She has relatives and friends either bugging her to death or not taking her calls. She has her own way and speed of handling things on her to-do list, and someone else might think their way is better than hers. It can get very messy, and your bride will need to come up for air every now and then, or she can get pulled apart.

Grooms usually don't see this part of the process. And it's not because they're insensitive or clueless . . . it's because they usually are more solution-oriented. When the bride's mother makes a sharp comment it may not even register with you, but it can cut your bride off at the knees. She is under pressure to do all of the following:

- Be true to her own wedding dreams and create the day she wants.
- Be true to your shared wedding dreams.
- Handle all the outside influences on the wedding, such as others' suggestions, others' demands, power plays, guilt trips, and absent involvement such as the mother who won't help if things aren't done her way. (Yes, some moms out there are not going to get the Mother of the Year award for this disheartening power play.)
- Make peace with the high cost of weddings, especially in today's tough economy. (How do you justify spending $1,000 on floral centerpieces when your job might be in jeopardy due to cutbacks and layoffs at the company?)
- Stay on top of her jam-packed schedule, with work, overtime, business travel, getting to the gym or yoga class, keeping up with friends and family, and spending time with you—there were not enough hours in the day *before* she took on the task of planning a wedding.

Your bride is stressed out, maybe sleep deprived, and living life like the silver ball in a pinball machine, getting pinged from this place to that at high speed. She might not be the relaxed little flower who always impressed you with her calmness, rational thought, and giving heart. Right now, she might need you to help keep her together, like she's kept you together during your most trying times.

Just remember that when she rips your head off about leaving the cap off the toothpaste.

Top 10 Rules
for Working with the Bride

1. *Listen well:* The worst thing you can do when she comes to you with her binder and clipboard, or when she fires up a spreadsheet on the computer and summons you to look at some plans she's considering for the reception, is tune out while you have one eye on the television and just say "Uh-huh" or "Yeah" or "Whatever you think, honey." She's going to smell your indifference. So listen well when it's time to talk wedding. That doesn't mean you have to drop everything when you're in the middle of an engrossing project just because she wants to talk details. It includes your right to ask her to sit down over coffee and discuss it at a planned time. She should give you that right as well.

2. *Respect her wishes:* She may have been dreaming about this wedding for a long time. You have to provide a certain amount of give when it comes to ideas she's obviously kept in a hope chest since she was nine years old. Sure, you can and should have your say about some things with the wedding, fully half if you're a 50–50 partner, but just be mindful of the things that are obviously nonnegotiable with her.

3. *Give her positive reinforcement . . . often:* I'm sure you already compliment her and treat her like gold. (You do, don't you? If not, get moving!) But she may need some extra TLC from you at this time. Consider her day: Her boss is pressuring her, her mother is stressing her, and she's spending more time eating Ben and Jerry's because they've never treated her badly. The woman could use some kindness right now, so be sure to kiss her in the morning and tell her she's beautiful. You can never do that too much, and brides really need to hear that you love them. Women are nervous about marriage too. That might be part of what has her so tense right now. You need to remember she's the woman you adore, and tell her that directly from time to time.

4. *Ask what you can do to help:* Again, this is something grooms don't realize, but brides *love* it when you show initiative and caring about the wedding. We love it when *you* show interest and ask *us* if you can help carry the load, rather than us always feeling like we have to bring it up with you. We don't want to be nags, even if you don't believe that.

5. *Don't shame her:* She's not happy that she's so stressed out. So reconsider your usual form of motivation, and don't criticize her or tell her that she's smarter than that, or she should be able to handle all this better.

6. *Take her out of the wedding world:* Too much of anything isn't a good thing, so if she's too wedding focused (which is easy to be), then you can be a hero and savior if you rescue her from the land of tulle and white roses and take her out for a beer, a wine, some sushi, an evening at a comedy club, or to a baseball game. Somewhere under all those wedding plans is the woman you enjoyed these things with, and she needs to return to *her*, not the bride-to-be version of her. Trust me on this . . . a good night out will relax her, and you could be on the receiving end of her good-mood reminder. And by this, I mean: Sex is a good way out of wedding stress—especially if you're generous.

7. *Let her vent:* She might need to get angry. So if she's storming around your place calling her jealous sister any number of R-rated words, let her vent. Don't try to put the lid back on that exploding pressure cooker. If you have to, take her to the driving range and let her whack some golf balls to get her frustrations out, or take her to the gym to hit the heavy bag. If you encourage her to get her anger out constructively, you'll be less likely to bear her wrath later.

8. *Be the go-to guy:* If she's got a full workload, but someone needs to drive an hour to go pick up the wine from the winery, be the guy who takes on that job. Or be the guy who'll pick up the relatives from the airport on the wedding weekend. Let her know that you're willing to save the day with these jobs, or that you can get your best man and groomsmen to help out if necessary. If your bride isn't skilled at delegating, she might not have taken the step of asking you for help. When you offer, you become her White Knight.

9. *Keep the big picture in mind:* Wedding planning is a finite process. It does come to an end. And in the end, it's all about the two of you getting married. It's very important for you to keep that in mind, and to remind her to keep that in mind as well. Others too. Someone has to have the clear head about the grand scheme of things, and the groom is very often just the right person to take her in an embrace and soothe her with a reminder that while the wedding is important, what's most important is that you're both going to be together. That the wedding is all about celebrating this.

10. *And finally . . . don't* ever say, *"Wow, honey. Are you PMSing right now?":* If you do that, *I'll* come slap you for her.

Working with Others

Unfortunately, you might find yourself in the position where your bride is a stress case, but she's nothing compared to the stress case her mother is . . . or your mother is. When planning a wedding, it seems everyone around you has deep, emotional connections to your wedding. Yes, they know it's your day, but if you could just do this one little thing the way it was done at their wedding . . . and if you could just have the wedding in a church because it would mean so much to your grandmother. . . .

It never ends. Your closest loved ones are going to want to have a hand in your wedding. There's a huge variation in *degree* of (okay, I'll say it) meddling, depending on your parents', family's, and friends' personalities, but you'd be a rare wedding couple to completely escape the threats of outside influence. And I also include all of your wedding vendors in this category, because many bridal professionals have their own ways of doing things. I know of brides who have been reduced to tears because a particularly flippant gown designer criticized her sense of style when she looked at a gown the designer thought would be unflattering to her. Everyone has a specific sensitivity level, and it can be frustrating to deal with those who lack diplomacy. That said, you can also be the hero for your bride if you help her navigate the interpersonal jungle that is wedding planning.

Be Aware!

Surprisingly *friends* can be one of the big stressors for brides and grooms. Depending on the individuals and their decency levels, you and your bride might feel that your friends have changed on you. For instance, she might have a close friend who now avoids her, or limits their girls' nights out, simply because that friend is envious of your fiancée's engaged status. For her own selfish reasons, that friend might be very catty about not wanting to hear all about the wedding. That can hurt your bride deeply. Or, your friends might be gigging you about becoming a boring married guy, saying that you're whipped, that you're *planning a wedding? What's wrong with you?* It's true that impending marriage does affect friendships, so be on the lookout for signs that your friends or your bride's friends are adding to your stress. When your life changes, so, too, does theirs, and they might need some time to adjust. Or *you* might need to be more yourself, as you were pre-engagement, to maintain old friendships.

Top 10 Tips for Working with Others to Plan Your Big Day (for You and Your Bride)

1. *Use your business skills:* Planning a wedding is a lot like handling a business acquisition or partnership. You'll need the well-honed office talents that have gotten you far in the corporate world in much the same way here: Bring out your negotiation skills, your ability to read people, your respectful assertiveness, your organization skills, accountability, integrity, and dependability. Know when a negotiation is stalled and when to take a different approach. Compromise. These skills of yours, and hers, are key to making it through this process in one piece.

2. *Ditch your old family roles:* It might be tough for you and your bride to treat parents, grandparents, and siblings like business colleagues in this shared task you have before you, especially if you're still in the hold of family roles and positions. I've seen the resolve of even the most together brides and grooms begin to waver when their fathers look annoyed or when their mothers whip up a batch of manicotti as a bargaining tool. Moments later, Mom and Dad have very smoothly gotten you over to their side of the fence, because you haven't taken an adult stance with them. This affects younger brides and grooms more often than older, more established couples, but I mention it here because moving out of childhood and family roles is an individual process—but a very important one when you're getting married. Right now is when you deliver the message to your families, if they haven't gotten it already, that you're to be dealt with in a respectful, adult way. And so is your bride. Families need to adjust to that, and this is the perfect time to make that distinction.

3. *Share your family-diplomacy secrets:* Make sure your bride knows that your mother doesn't respond well to a certain kind of communication, or that your father will agree with anything if he doesn't feel like he's been *told* what to do. Even at an adult-dealings level, you still know how your family works. So be sure to clue in your bride, and ask the

same of her, so that all future dealings with them on this new planning level will go more smoothly.

4. *Present a united front:* Let everyone else know from the outset that you're planning this wedding as a team, and all decisions will be made by the two of you. Others need to know that you're a part of the package too.

5. *Never play the middleman:* Others can be tricky about sliding their "suggestions" to the bride through you. So if your mother tells you to "work on her" about the whole band versus deejay argument for the reception, you should refuse. Establishing yourself as her leverage tool is a fatal mistake that can have very negative effects on your relationship with your bride. It keeps your mother safe and puts you in the danger zone. So refuse to pass messages along except in benign cases, and encourage your mother to speak directly with her future daughter-in-law. They need to learn to work together, to accept each other's wishes.

6. *Defend your bride:* If said meddling mother takes a solid sucker punch at your bride's character, step up and let her know that kind of trash talking is just not going to fly with you. Stop it the first time, and your mother will likely get the message that she can't speak that way about the woman you love. This applies to everyone you deal with, including friends who don't want you to leave the bachelors' circle.

7. *Know and uphold your priorities:* All the way through, hang on to what you most want for your wedding.

8. *Make the process enjoyable:* This is supposed to be *fun.* If you, she, or both of you start to take this whole thing too seriously, then it's a burden and not a blessing. So whatever you do, keep the laughter going each step of the way. As convoluted as the wedding planning process is, there is a *lot* to poke fun at in a good-natured way.

9. *Keep others in the loop:* Especially if both sets of parents are helping to pay for the wedding, share all the good news about the wedding plans, and let others enjoy it.

10. *Never, ever complain about the wedding or your bride to anyone else:* Discretion is key. And what you say to others might come back to haunt you. Remember what I said about brides remembering the planning stage forever? If she hears that you called her a bitch (even if you're right and she's acting like one), you'll have a mark on your permanent record.

There's no perfect way to interact and to work with others during the planning of a wedding because everyone is different. We all handle things our own ways, some better and more rational than others, and we all have our own breaking points. But if you appoint yourself as the guy who keeps your bride relaxed, the guy who ensures that everyone treats you and your bride respectfully, this entire process is going to be much more enjoyable and much less stressful for everyone. Share this chapter with your bride right now, and open up a conversation in which she'll feel free to ask you directly for what she needs from you. Together, you can locate any trouble spots with others, and you can create a game plan for handling anyone who acts up along the way.

I've said it already several times in this book, but it's worth repeating: Planning a wedding is great preparation for marriage. Right now is your training ground for the road ahead, and even if you fight during the process, it's all good because you get to practice fighting fair in times of great stress. Passions may flare, and both of you might not be too proud of yourselves when you've taken a wrong step with each other, but apologies are vital for the future of your relationship. So this crazy time of interpersonal struggle might be the best thing for the two of you. You'll learn to work better together in a unique time of challenge, and you'll also learn what you both need to work on to create a stronger partnership. It's the two of you against the world, some might say, so it's best to get your plan together. Planning a wedding is a bonding experience for both of you, and for family and friends involved in the process. It's something you'll always share.

And when you take your vows, when you repeat the part about "for richer and for poorer, for better and for worse, in sickness and in health," you already have many months of introductory experience from the planning time.

So keep in mind for now and for the future . . . the correct answer is "Yes, dear."

II

The Details

7

◇ ◇ ◇

What You're Wearing

YOUR BRIDE loves the way you look in a suit. We women love our men dressed sharply, smooth, and very sexy in a great suit or tuxedo, and your challenge right now is to find *the* best wedding day wardrobe for you, for your men, for your dads, and for the little guys in your bridal party. You want a smart and sophisticated look, great fashion sense, and a flattering cut . . . but also a style that works perfectly with the style of your wedding as a whole. Elegant wedding = elegant look for you, as well as for your bride. And men do "elegant" in a prescribed way for weddings.

Fashion might not be your forte—perhaps you'll leave the whole tux-selection thing to your bride—but if you're even the least bit involved with choosing your formalwear, you'll need to know the ins and outs of men's outfitting for the big day.

Read on to learn the following: the rules of formality; style tips for your outfit, shoes, and accessories; the task of coordinating tux rentals and returns; and even some tips on getting great designer tuxes or suits for less money.

Just a Formality

The formality and style of your wedding dictates the selection of what you will wear. Obviously, a five-star formal wedding calls for classy tuxedoes, while a more informal wedding style will put your men in chino's and crisp white dress shirts for that beach wedding overlooking the ocean. Each wedding has its fashion rules, and you want to fit into the grand scheme by dressing appropriately.

Luckily for you, the world of men's formalwear has recently taken a giant leap forward from the days when you rented your first tuxedo to wear to the prom. Fabrics are lighter and higher-quality with a great sheen and more flattering cuts (to make your shoulders look solid and even giving you the look of more height), top designers have entered the ring with their own lines of tuxes, and accessories run the gamut from long black jackets (a hot look right now!) to theme-printed vests, matching ties and shirts, and celebrity-stoked fashions. More attention is paid to what the wedding-day men will wear, too. So you are on the receiving end of a wider and greater variety of fashion opportunities than ever. (Trust me, once you start trying on tuxes and see the impressed look in your bride's eyes as you're modeling that Armani for her, you'll grow a little more attached to the subject than you might be right now.)

The degree of formality is the big issue. Logically you'll start off your wardrobe search by knowing exactly what the formality level of your wedding is, since you can't choose a tux or suit without knowing that. Here are the rules to choose by:

Ultraformal Evening (commonly called "white tie")

- Black tailcoat
- White tailcoat or waistcoat
- Wing-collared white shirt
- White vest or black vest
- White bow tie (tie and vest are in matching color, whether black or white)
- Black patent-leather shoes
- Cufflinks in gold or silver
- Optional white gloves

Ultraformal Daytime

- Black or gray waistcoat or gray cutaway coat
- Gray pants or gray pinstriped pants

  or . . .
- Gray cutaway tuxedo
- White wing-collar shirt
- Gray vest
- Gray solid or striped ties

  or . . .
- Ascot (optional)

- Black patent-leather shoes

  or . . .
- Spats
- Gold or silver cufflinks
- Gloves (optional)

Formal evening (commonly called "black tie")

- Black tuxedo or tailcoat

  or . . .
- Black stroller coat
- White wing-collar shirt
- Black bow tie or long tie
- Black cummerbund or vest
- Black patent-leather shoes
- Gold, silver, or black cufflinks

  or . . .
- Black tuxedo pants
- White or off-white dinner jacket or cutaway jacket
- Black tie
- Black patent-leather shoes
- Cufflinks and other classy accents

Formal Daytime

- Gray cutaway tuxedo

  or . . .
- Gray jacket with gray pinstriped pants

  or . . .
- Black or gray morning coat with gray waistcoat and black-and-gray pinstriped pants (very classy!)

  or . . .
- Light-colored or white jacket
- White spread-collar shirt or white wing-collar shirt
- Ties or vests in color or coordinating print, such as a black-and-gray striped tie
- Black shoes
- Cufflinks

Semiformal Evening

- Black tuxedo or suit

  or . . .
- White dinner jacket with formal black pants
- White or slightly hued wing-collar or turned-down-collar shirt
- Black or color-coordinated long tie
- Color-coordinated vest or cummerbund
- Black shoes

Semiformal Daytime

- Gray stroller coat

  or . . .
- Navy or gray suits

  or . . .

- White linen suit in summer
  or . . .
- Gray, navy, or black jacket
- White shirt
- Color-coordinated full-length (or four-in-hand) tie (optional)
- Gray vest
- Suit-friendly shoes

Informal Daytime

- Gray, navy, or tan suit with white shirt
  or . . .
- Navy blazer and white shirt with khaki pants
  or . . .
- White button-down shirt with khaki pants

- Solid or patterned, color-coordinating tie (optional)
- Suitable shoes to match outfit (no white shoes, please!)

Informal Evening

- Dark suits with white shirts and coordinating ties
- Dark shoes

Ultra-Informal

- Khaki pants or shorts with white or hued button-down shirts
- Bathing suit on the beach
- Suitable shoes, or barefoot to match your bride

Tuxedoes

If the formality rules of your formal, ultraformal, or semiformal wedding say *it's going to be a tuxedo*, then here's where you start your search for the *right* tuxedo. Undoubtedly, your bride has already flipped through several (dozen) bridal magazines by the time you get to this subject, so she might already have a packet of torn-out pictures of the tuxedo styles that will work well to match her style of gown. If so, then half of your work is already done. From these pages, you might hit the Internet to check out these designers' Web sites, as well as the most popular wedding Web sites with must-know details about tuxedo elements. My favorites, which I recommend for browsing, are:

- ModernBride.com
- BridalGuide.com
- WeddingChannel.com

And for a complete primer on all things tuxedoes, go to www.formalwear.org. That is where you'll find highly detailed definitions and explanations of men's style points, such as single-breasted jackets with one button. . . . double-breasted with two, four, or six buttons. . . . shawl lapels . . . strollers . . . cutaways . . . band collars . . . the list goes on and on in great detail.

Of course, the menswear style consultant you choose at the rental agency or department store (more on this later!) will certainly be able to guide your choices, but it's always good to have at least a general grasp of the terms and style categories so that you can be an informed consumer and not some sales clerk's dress-up doll. The more you know about the wide-ranging world of men's tuxedoes, collars, shirts, and so on, the better your ability to work *with* any salesperson to find the look that's *you*.

On the Web

At this time, it's a great idea to look through the individual Web sites or search in stores for designer tuxedo styles and details, for an even deeper look into today's hottest menswear styles. Here are a few of the top names in men's formalwear for you to consider:

After Hours Formalwear	Fumigalli's
After Six Formalwear	Tommy Hilfiger
Claiborne	Calvin Klein
Essentials Collection	Ralph Lauren (one line
FUBU (*great* urban-inspired	is Chaps)
tuxedoes and accessories!)	Frederick Leone
Geoffrey Beene (one line is FCGI)	Lord West
Hartz	Lubiam
Hugo Boss	Montreaux
Oscar de la Renta	PBM
Christian Dior	Pegeen
Perry Ellis	Raffinati and Rheingold
Andrew Fezza	Tallia Uomo

Get Your Timing Right!

Remember, this isn't the prom, so you can't leave the tuxedo search until two weeks before the wedding like you did when you were seventeen. Like your bride, you'll need to start looking *early*, in order to allow yourself time to find the right style of tuxedo, assemble a group order for your men, and be sure that you're reserving the best tuxedo out there in plenty of time to assure it will be available on your wedding weekend. Especially in peak wedding months (late spring to early fall), not to mention prom time in May, when hundreds of young men in your area are going to be slipping into tuxes for their own big nights out, demand is high and the top tuxes rent out early. So, to give yourselves the best chance of landing your top pick, get to work on this *at least* six months before the wedding. The very latest date to order would be around the three-month mark. I kid you not . . . tuxedo rental requires early action.

The preceding is true, unless you're buying a tuxedo, which is a more and more popular option these days. If your social schedule and society circle might bring you to formal events such as fundraisers, premieres, the opera, and additional ultraformal weddings in your group of family, friends, and colleagues, then it might be a wise investment to buy your tuxedo. Read this chapter and check tuxedo Web sites in order to choose your desired style and designer, and then pursue your stylish purchase for all your future formal events. A style consultant at the store or designer's salon will help you with the particulars for your shape, height, and coloring, plus the selection of an evergreen style that will last beyond this season alone. And be sure to go to a salon itself for custom measuring. While you can certainly buy a tux over the Internet, the lack of personalized service makes this an unwise move.

Going to the Experts: Finding the Best Tuxedo Rental Agency

Like everything else in the wedding world, *where* you shop and who you work with is crucial to the best outcome. This means that you have to find the best tuxedo rental store out there. Sure, there's one in every shopping mall and on plenty of Main Streets, which must mean they're all pretty much the same, right?

Wrong. You should never choose a tuxedo rental agency based on its proximity to your home. Instead of the closest, you need to make sure you're choosing the best . . . an agency with a long-standing reputation for fine service, qualified and knowledgeable fashion consultants to help select tuxes and measure you well, reliability of service and delivery, and—most important—top-quality merchandise. That means the latest styles of tuxedoes on the market, and not the same dusty jackets and pants they offered back in 1987.

The best shops out there welcome you like a prized client, not a number. They'll answer your questions, show you dozens of styles if you can't quite find the right one, and they stock an enormous selection of suitable suits, plus accessories and shoes to rent. The best shops out there will have you dealing with a friendly and attentive rental agent who will ask questions about the wedding's location and style your bride's gown, the season of your wedding, and whether it will be indoors or outside. You'll be asked for your budget level and presented with workable options in your range. This third-degree drilling is a sign that you're working with a seasoned operation.

Once the choice is made, you will be custom measured and fitted for the most flattering hang of the jacket and length of pants, and you'll be offered multiple choices in vests, shirts, cummerbunds, ties, and accessories for a well-pulled-together look your bride will love. The best shops and the best style agents out there will make you comfortable throughout the process. These pros know how to make even the manliest of men much less self-conscious checking out his back view in the mirror and deciding between silk and satin ties.

So how do you choose a tuxedo rental agency? How do you know which place has that attentive and quick-to-coordinate stylist, the best designer tuxes, and all the gear you'll need? Your first step is to ask recently married friends which tux shop they used, and see how happy they were with their choice. Clients of mine tell me their search was quickly and easily stopped after a resounding referral from friends. Word-of-mouth is the best assurance out there, since the shop has proven its worth to people whose tastes are like your own. Of course, you'll need to take this referral into consideration and still go check out the shop itself, meet with the style coordinator, and get your own feel for how comfortable you are there and how much you like their stock. Nothing beats in-person scouting.

If you have no recently married friends or family on your speed dial, you'll need to invest more time and energy into your search. Your first step should be checking with a formalwear rental association to get the names, addresses, and contact information of local, highly-rated rental agencies. This is just an information-gathering exercise, since you never want to take what you read on a Web site as gospel. Use this information to create a list of possibilities, and then set out to "interview" the store, its stock, and its stylist.

On the Web

For formalwear-store ratings, check the International Formalwear Association at www.formalwear.org. Membership in this society is an additional green flag for any agency you're considering, since association members need to be well-rated, established for a certain number of years, and owners and staff are certain to be trained and have access to the latest and greatest information in tuxedo design and styles. Membership is *not* an automatic referral, but it is a plus sign.

Also, many of the bridal Web sites listed on page 72 also provide local vendor tools where you can point-and-click your way to rental-agency suggestions. Although these are not necessarily association-approved vendors, it will nevertheless provide a list of choices.

Once you've collected your list of potential shops to check out, whether through Web site research or friends' referrals, or even through an advertisement in a local paper's special wedding section, set aside a few days to personally check them out.

Scoping the Shop

Here's what you're looking for when you cruise through a formalwear rental shop:

- A wide range of designer high-end and moderate-end tuxedoes
- A wide range of tuxedoes in different styles and colors

- Well-organized and attractive surroundings
- Brochures or printed price packages including full details
- Acceptable rental fees, and special discounts offered for grooms (Such as "Rent 5 tuxedoes, get the groom's free!")
- Attentive and well-mannered sales associates
- How busy the shop is on a Thursday or Friday

This last one is important, since it would be wise to check out how other grooms and their groomsmen are being served as they're coming in to pick up their orders. Are the guys standing around kicking at the carpet, steaming because they've been waiting an hour for a tux order that was supposed to be ready? Watch for real-life interaction, listen in on conversations between the rental agents and real customers, and suss out the overall vibe of the place.

They're Looking at *You*, Too

Upon meeting with a formalwear rental associate, he or she will assess your wedding's size, style, formality, and location in order to select the most appropriate tuxedo, but the other part of this assessment is a good long look at you. Some tuxedo designs are better for taller men, some better for shorter and broader men. Some jackets flatter guys with a bit of a beer belly, and others make a thinner appearance look stockier. Your *men* should also be assessed for their heights and builds. Smart engaged couples bring in photos of the groomsmen and ushers for the rental agent to see, just to give an idea of the range of heights and body shapes in your group. Looking at the range gives your formalwear agent a good handle on the best tuxedo style to make you all look great.

This Fabric Is So Soft

The fabric of tuxedoes is probably the last thing on your mind, but you should know that a lighter-weight fabric is going to be better in the hot summer months, while a heavier fabric is fine for more moderate weather. If you've seen grooms or groomsmen melting in their tuxes at other weddings, particularly outdoor

Tuxedoes for Less Money

Here are some money-saving tips for getting a better deal on your tuxedoes and accessories:

- Ask about discount packages. Some shops run specials on certain designers' tuxes, and you might be able to get in on a good deal for that Ralph Lauren.

- Negotiate for a free tux for you (or for the father of the bride, to score big points) with your large order of tux rentals. Many shops offer a freebie when you rent five, six, eight, or ten tuxes.

- If you can't get a discount on the tux rental using your powers of persuasion, then ask for free add-ins, such as no-charge cummerbund, bow tie, and shoe rentals. You'll be surprised at how willing these wedding-based pros are to make you happy on the price, so you might get some freebies if you ask.

- Check out any partnership deals. Those coupons at the register might be junk, but they also might be certificates for discounts on boutonnieres at the local florist who is partnering with that shop. So don't pass anything by without looking at it first.

- Choose tuxes made from fabrics that are less expensive to rent. (Yes, we're back to fabrics again!) Top-quality tuxes usually come in fabrics marked as *super* 110's and 120's, which is the number of threads per inch. These higher thread counts are often a sign of a higher quality, more attractive tux that holds its shape better, and as with all things in higher-end, top-quality fashion, they cost more. The average tuxedo has a 60 to 75 thread count, but you might find these suits to be a bit downscale. Aim for a mid-range thread count of 90 to 100 (called "Super 100's") for great quality at a more moderate price. Or use your savvy negotiating skills to get those top of the line 110's or 120's for a bargain if you get other items in your order for free or at discount.

- Sometimes, gray or white tuxedoes cost less than those very *in* black tuxedoes. Check price points between the options and see if that charcoal gray tuxedo would work for your event's style.

- Be honest with your stylist about your budget limitations and concerns. These pros work with budget-conscious grooms more often than not, and they undoubtedly have a long list of more moderately priced but still great-looking tuxes.

weddings, you'll understand why I'm bringing this up. You might even have been one of those sweat-soaked groomsmen yourself in the past.

Your tux rental agent is going to steer you to the right fabrics for the date and season of your wedding, choosing among wools, linens, and other good fabrics for the weather. He or she might have fabric samples on hand to show you. Choosing the right fabric for comfort as well as appearance is key. Note: "120's" are great for year-round weather, so you might just want to stick with that fine selection to make your life easier.

When you're on a tight budget, you might think that you'll be relegated to the crappiest tuxes in the place, but that's not true. Some shops keep last season's Perry Ellis tuxedoes around at something of a discount so you can still get into a designer tux at a lower price. This brings up a point I want to stress: Don't assume that a tux rental agent is trying to squeeze extra money out of you by bringing out designer tuxes. Like most fashion experts, their eye is on which style would be best for you and your event, and they know that a certain designer tux will just look better on you. They want the suit to hold its shape, hang just right, present well in a trademark shinier fabric. They're going for quality, and they want to keep you out of the low-budget suits that just look like, well, a cheaper suit. Trust your stylist's input and consider these slightly pricier models for their great sheen, their great fit, and their great cut. How you look in the tux is what matters. And remember, even if you have to go a bit above your planned budget for your tuxedoes, there are *plenty* of other places in your wedding budget where you can make up the difference.

Tuxedo Terminology

Here is where you learn the basic terminology in tuxedo jackets, vests, shirts, and so on. Again, your tux rental agent can show you the different types of collars and jackets right there in person, but you can check at www.formalwear.org, www.theknot.com, and various other bridal and formalwear sites for an initial overview of the different tuxedo element styles, as well as primers on which types of collars work with which types of tuxedoes. It's an art, a science, and a fashionably enforced code of proper dressing, so do your research and be able to at least follow along while your stylist discusses the following:

Jackets

- Two-button tuxedo
- Single-button tuxedo
- Three-button tuxedo
- Single-breasted tuxedo
- Double-breasted tuxedo
- Shawl-collar tuxedo
- Notch lapel, features a sideways V-shaped cutout at collar level
- Peak lapel, accent points upward and outward just below collar level
- Shawl lapel
- Classic stroller jacket
- Full-dress tailcoat
- Dinner jacket
- Cutaway jacket (also called a morning coat)
- Waistcoat (jacket without the tails)

Pants

- Adjustable-waist tuxedo pants
- Nonadjustable waist
- Fabrics in polyester or 100 percent wool
- Striped or pinstriped
- Cuffed bottom or non-cuff

Shirts

- Wing-collar formal
- Spread-collar formal

How About a Skirt?

Don't forget the option of a plaid kilt if you want to honor your heritage with traditional Scottish dress. Some cultural costumes also ditch the formal pants and put you in a robe or different kind of bottoms. Explore ethnic-dress possibilities through an Internet search, through cultural associations, and at heritage festivals.

- Crossed-collar formal
- Informal folded collar
- Laydown or turndown collar
- Mandarin-band collar
- Crossover collar
- Cavalier bands, have a pleated chest front
- French cuffs
- Pleating
- Silk microfiber blends
- 100 percent cotton

Vests

- 5–8-button vests
- Fullback vests, completely cover the back
- Open-backed vests, attach around the waist
- 100 percent silk vests
- Color-coordinated shiny or patterned fabrics

- Color-coordinated vest and tie sets
- Deep colors look best; blush pastels are doable, but men look better in darker hues
- Geometric patterns

- Optional theme designs such as shamrocks, wine bottles, chili peppers, golf clubs, for a personalized and fun look
- Adjustable inside belts
- Besom pockets

In place of a vest, you can wear a high-style cummerbund around your waist—and it goes on with the pleating facing *up*, not down. Look for traditional and lantana style (lantana has a notched bottom and unique wrap).

A Dash of Color

Vest and tie sets now come in a wide range of colors, from black to champagne, lavender, silver, sapphire, bordeaux, red, rose, white, and on through the color spectrum. Very hot right now are the metallic sheen vest and tie sets—from black to gold, platinum and ice blue, these vests have some shine and complement the hot new styles in bridesmaids' dresses—so your men can look twenty-first-century as well. Patterns are diverse, so you'll surely find a vest ensemble with a stylish flair.

Ties

- Classic bow ties in 100 percent silk or silk blends
- Pre-tied, adjustable bow ties with easy-clasps in back.
- 100 percent silk or silk-blend long ties
- Ascots
- Bolo ties (very trendy right now!)

Shoes

- Formal, black patent-leather shoes
  or . . .
- Matte-finish formal leather shoes
- Rounded shoe toe boxes or slightly squared toe boxes
- Wing-tip
- All men's shoes, ideally, should match exactly

- Very important: Matching black socks for all your men!
- Socks can be solid or slightly patterned in a stylish design—uniformity is key!

Tip: Socks are the number-one wardrobe problem for groomsmen. Have your best man get three extra pairs of socks and bring them along on the wedding day for dressing time.

Accessories

- Gold or silver cufflinks or studs
- Black onyx cufflinks and studs
- Diamond- or rhinestone-accent cufflinks and studs
- Laser-cut cufflinks and studs
- Alumni-print cufflinks and studs (order from your alumni association)
- Antique-cut cufflinks
- Classic black silk buttoncovers (with or without gemstone accents)
- Pocket squares
- Suspenders
- Top hats (in black, white, or gray)
- "Zoot"-style hats, as in the 1930s–1940s swing-band-era style (see www.zootsuitstore.com for examples) when men are wearing zoot suits for a theme wedding
- Canes
- Gloves

Formal and Informal Suits

If your wedding will not be formal, you might not need to dive into the world of tuxedoes at all. Some of the more laid-back weddings that are very popular these days might prescribe less formal attire for both your bride and you. In these cases, such as an informal outdoor wedding, a Sunday brunch, an at-home gathering

More Money-Saving Tips for the Men's Wardrobe

- Choose all-inclusive packages, such as those that include discounts or freebies on alterations, accessories, and shoe rentals.

- If you can't swing the price of a designer tuxedo, have your tux rental agent present you with the best-quality basic tuxedoes possible.

- Go with classic, elegant styles and stay away from the hot new trends in men's wedding-day fashion, which can be marked up due to their popularity.

- Consider using color in the men's wedding-day wardrobe. If the shop rents more basic black options to the majority of their wedding clientele, ask if the colored ties, vests, and cummerbunds are marked down due to lower demand.

- Have your bride check if her bridal-gown salon provides a partnership discount on tux rentals. Your fiancée might be able to net you a better deal when partnered with her gown purchase.

- Shop at designer menswear outlets and department store sales for great prices on shirts and accessories.

that's more family style than formal style, dark suits for the guys might be just the ticket.

If this is your situation, you'll be happy to know that you might already have a great suit in your closet that gives you a free ride and an already proven stylish look for the wedding day. Or, you and your men may need to hit the department stores to get great, coordinating black or deep navy suits. Whatever your call, you *must* make sure that all of your men's suits match precisely—since one man's navy could be another man's cobalt blue. Range in coloring for men's suits can vary by designer, and you don't want your guys looking like a poorly matched set. The same goes for the "wear chinos or khaki pants" directive to your men. Colors in khakis range from a beige to almost a greenish hue. So be sure to coordinate a shopping trip, or have all your guys bring their suits over to your place for a quick check by you and your bride. It might be that *none* of you need to shell out for anything more than crisp white shirts with matching collars and a chosen tie style.

All the Same Shirt

I know this is a lot of attention to detail that might not even be on your radar, but uniformity for your men's wedding-day look is incredibly important. Be sure to arrange for *all* of them to buy the exact same style and brand of shirt. Again, designs and colors of "white dress shirts" vary, and collar style is a key factor for matching up your men's wedding-day look. Get your guys' shirt sizes, lengths, and neck measurements so that you, or your best man, can go pick up those dress shirts at one time.

Shoes

Your men need to be in similar shoe styles and colors, and you need to specify this quite clearly . . . including your wishes for their socks! Some "in control" brides have asked their grooms and men to come by the house for a shoe review, where they looked at the men's shoes to be sure the chosen styles would look good on the big day. No ratty heels, scuffs, or obviously old shoes will do. Your bride might not be so selective, but you should avoid a footwear fiasco on the wedding day by making your shoe wishes clear to your men. They can visit discount shoe stores or take advantage of department store sales that you or your bride can alert them about in order to nudge them to buy a new pair of shoes.

Casual and Beachwear

If your wedding will be very casual, then you might decide to wear (and have your men wear as well) a simple pair of khaki shorts and a short-sleeve white dress shirt for a casual-smart look at a relaxed wedding. Some grooms break out the Hawaiian shirts for their fun beach or poolside weddings, and others step into their bathing suits for a very laid-back beach-lovers' ceremony. In this case, the style of dress for your men just needs to be decided upon and disseminated to your guys.

"You Need Professional Help"

If a group suit-shopping trip is in order, be sure to call your chosen menswear department ahead of time to schedule a personalized, assisted shopping expedition. The store's stylist can better handle your large group if he or she knows you're coming in, and you'll be almost certain of netting a nice per-person discount for your group purchase.

Want to Stand Out?

In years past, grooms were happy to stand out from their crowd of groomsmen and ushers simply by wearing a different type of flower in their lapels. Or, they wore a white vest with a white bow tie rather than the black vest and tie ensemble their men were wearing. Now, today's groom wants to go a step farther and *really* stand out from the pack. While wearing a different color tux is a definite *don't*, you can check out the following options for groom originality:

- Very popular now is going global and wearing ceremonial wedding attire or robes of such ethnic backgrounds as Africa, Korea, Russia, and so on.
- The groom wears a coordinating color vest or a vest in a solid color, his men wear a pattern.
- The groom wears a metallic-sheen vest; his men wear standard hues.
- The groom wears a classy cutaway coat; his men wear regular tuxedo jackets.
- The groom wears a jacket with satin lapels; his men's jackets have plain lapels.
- The groom wears a white bow tie; his men wear long white or colored ties, or standard black bow ties.
- The groom wears his military uniform (if applicable); the rest of his men wear tuxedoes.
- The groom wears a standard white dress shirt; his men wear pleated-front shirts.
- The groom wears a shirt with a fold-down or wing collar; his men wear shirts with banded collars.

One of the sharpest collections of wedding men I've ever seen wore black jackets with black band collars and shiny cufflinks and studs. The groom set himself apart by wearing gold accents while his men wore black. It was a smooth look their crowd loved, as was evidenced by the number of guests clamoring to take pictures of just the men. Who knew when they'd all look so good again?! One of the men's wives came to me and said she wished her husband would look that good more often and that she was completely hot for him right then. Never underestimate the power of a great black tuxedo with modern style.

Getting Everyone Outfitted

Once you have chosen the style of tuxedo or suit and placed it in the final decision category of your wedding plans, it's time to round up your men and get them ready for the big order. However, these days, your men might live all over the country, even overseas. You might not all be in the same state until a few days before the wedding. So how do you arrange the order if no one is in the same time zone? It's a matter of having your men go to *get professionally measured by a qualified tailor*. I've emphasized this because it's crucial for them to get their measurements taken by a pro who knows how to measure arm length. Problems arise when guys get out their measuring tapes and attempt to save themselves the embarrassment of getting their guts measured by someone else. Homegrown measurements make for horribly fitted tuxes. So put it in strict terms: Go to a tailor! (Note: They might have to pay a small fee for a measurement, but it's money well spent when their tuxes are flattering on the big day.)

You'll instruct each of your men to go to the pro and have a size card filled out (see example below). All of his crucial digits will be listed there in official recording, and then the men can either fax it to you, e-mail you their sizes, or

---

Sample Size Card

While most shops use their own formatted size cards, this sample shows the required measurements:

Name: _____

Address: _____

Phone Number: _____

E-mail: _____

Shirt Size: Waist:

Neck Size: Inseam:

Sleeve Length: Shoe Size:

---

bring the card along with them when it's time to order. No matter how they deliver the information, they need to deliver the *right* information.

The ideal formalwear rental agency will provide the work of an expert who knows the correct length of sleeves (the end of the jacket reaches to the top of the hand, for instance) and allows for good range of movement in the shoulders. Your men should be able to sit, stand, and hug someone comfortably without their jackets pulling unnaturally or restricting their range of motion. Your formalwear pro will know to order the tux that fits each man's largest dimension, whether it's his chest, waist, or (hopefully not!) butt. That larger size can be tailored down for the best fit with the least amount of extra seam work, while a too-small tux presents a big dilemma that could have at least one of your men looking more like an overstuffed sausage than the dashing groomsman he could be in a better suit.

When those size cards are in, and your formalwear rental agent has had the opportunity to ask you about your men's general builds and height, you can then place the one bulk order at your agency. Your men need to pay up for their deposits and be ready with their checkbooks or credit cards for the final payment on pickup, so get your best man in gear as the organizer of the group payment process.

Dads and Sons

The fathers of the bride and groom usually dress to match you and your guys, so that might mean tuxedoes for them as well. Since the dads are going the formal route along with you, why not encourage them to stand apart as well? For instance, they might wear gray vests and ties to stand out from the bridal party's black or white ones, or they can go snazzy with those metallic silver vests. Originality and fashion flair are not just for the young set, so ask the dads if they have a preference for a style all their own.

As for the opposite end of the age spectrum—your ring bearers—the little guys can go full-out with rented tuxedoes as well. Formalwear shops usually stock a wide range of mini-versions of men's tuxedoes, complete with size-appropriate ties, cummerbunds, shoes, and accessories. So if the parents can swing the rental fees, then this is both a classy and cute way to outfit your boys. Other options for the smallest guys at less formal weddings are allowing them to wear black dress pants and white dress shirts, and then popping matching ties or bow ties on them. At really informal weddings, the boys can wear khaki shorts and a dress shirt to match your men exactly.

Save Money for Kids' Parents

Budget-Saving Tips for the Parents of the Ring Bearers

- Ask for the ring bearer's tux for free, rather than yours, as part of a large order; this is a way to give a break to the child's parents. You can afford to rent your own tux. Getting a freebie is a nice gesture for already-generous parents of the tykes.
- Suggest to ring bearers' parents that they get dress pants and shirts for the boys during clothing sales . . . such as the children's formalwear sales that happen after the winter holidays and Easter. (Note: The flowergirls' parents are onto this one as well, shopping for the girls' formal dresses during these big sell-offs of party dresses.)
- Let parents of child attendants know where the nearest outlet stores are—if they don't know already—for great deals on kids' partywear.
- Point out that kids don't need to get new shoes. If their black dress shoes fit, that's fine for them, or . . . parents can shop for the boys' new dress shoes at a discount shoe store and probably find a pair for under $20.

When you're choosing something for your ring bearers to wear, keep in mind that comfort is key. Look for light fabrics that will keep kids cool even in the hot summer months. A hot child is a cranky child, and an itchy child is a tantrum waiting to happen. So look for high-quality cotton-blend fabrics with cotton linings, rather than nylon or other less breathable materials. Stay away from anything that pinches, binds, itches, or pulls, and make sure the little guys will at least stay in their jackets until the ceremony is over. Smart couples allow their kids to peel off a layer after the major pictures are done, and some couples even allow the kids to change into more comfy clothes during the reception.

Placing the Final Order

With your men's sizes in, the dads' styles and sizes pulled together, and your ring bearer's rental order ready to roll, you can place your order with the tux rental shop. When you're filling out your order form, be sure you have *all* of the following information in print on the form to ensure that you get everything you need. Double-check the accuracy of the measurements for each man on your list, and improve your odds of no hassles when the order arrives.

Here's what you need to record:

- Your name and full contact information as the point person for the order
- The name and number of the sales associate who helped you
- The wedding date and time
- The names of all the groomsmen and ushers
- Individual, itemized sizes for each order
- The name of the tuxedo designer
- The tuxedo style number
- The exact thread count and fabric of the tuxedo
- Specific style names or numbers of all accessories, such as ties, vests, cummerbunds, and so on.
- Specific color names of all colored items, such as "bordeaux," "metallic silver," "rose," "midnight black," and so on.
- The style name and number of rented shoes
- All shoe sizes
- Deposit amount marked *paid* (Very important! Have the shop sign off on your deposits as *paid* to avoid discrepancy, double-payment, or small claims court later on.)
- Final payment amount and due date
- Pickup date and time
- Required return date and time (Very important! In some cases, returning the tuxes after noon counts as "a day late," with a hefty extra charge for each tux returned after the clock strikes. So be sure that the man who returns all the tuxes and accessories after the wedding is aware of the time on the order form.)

- Late return fee details and exact charges incurred
- Cancellation policy and refund rules
- Signature of formalwear consultant

Pickup and Delivery

A few days before the wedding, you and all of your men will go to the formalwear rental agency to try on and pick up your tuxedoes. At this last-minute meeting, the suits for your guys might need a little tweaking and tucking, especially if they haven't been tried on, but instead selected from size cards. Some formalwear shops arrange to have you or your guys come in four or five days before the wedding in case extra alterations are needed, so it is smart to let your agent know if and when your far-flung groomsmen will be coming into town. Separate try-on appointments might be necessary.

Once you slip into that tux and everything looks great, you're good to go. Just be sure to gather up your tie and accessories and your shoes if you're renting them.

The Big Returns

As mentioned earlier, someone is going to have to return all of the tuxedoes and accessories after the wedding. Appoint a dependable return guy to take on this task. It could be your best man or a brother-in-law who's volunteered, or it could be one of the fathers who steps in when your men's travel schedules mean they can't swing out to the rental agency the morning after the wedding. Whomever you tap for the job, make sure he knows what's to be returned—including shoes, rented cufflinks, pocket squares, gloves, and so on.

Dressing on the Wedding Day

Now I'm going to cover your wedding-morning preparations. Usually the groom and his men get together at his place or at a hotel room where they all get dressed and ready for the day ahead, so you'll need to let your guys know where the prep work will take place. Supply breakfast (or lunch) and coffee for them, and if alcohol is part of this pre-wedding gathering be sure to keep consumption low. Your bride and her girls might be sipping on champagne or mimosas that morning as they prepare to head off to the beauty salon, but it's pretty unlikely that anyone over there is doing shots or sucking whiskey out of a flask to calm her nerves.

That day, you'll be prepped and primed with a good haircut you've gotten a few days before the wedding and a nice close shave; some grooms tell me they go to the gym for a good workout just to clear their heads for the wedding ahead. Some guys play golf that morning, some toss a football around, and others sit down with their video games to zone out for a little while. By now, that mental break might be just what you need.

When the clock strikes time to get dressed, your best man might stand by to tell you if your tie is straight and your cummerbund flipped the right way, and he'll also help you find your shoes. Don't be surprised if your hands are shaking a bit while you're tying your bow tie or buttoning your jacket. This is a *big* event you're dressing for, and even pure excitement can register as something close to fear. So depend on your buddies to lighten things up for you, and hang in there. The best is yet to come.

Husband-of-the-Year Award

The best thing you can do that morning as you're dressing for the wedding is to keep your bride in mind. Somewhere across town, she's getting her hair, nails, and makeup done, and she might be shaking a bit herself. The best grooms out there arrange to have a wedding gift, flowers, or a personal note delivered to the bride before the big moment. And don't forget to call her on her cell phone to tell her you love her. She'll remember that forever.

Last-Second Tux Problems

Since you can always expect the unexpected at a wedding, you might be one of those grooms with a big tux crisis on the morning of the wedding. If the back seam of your jacket rips when your beefier cousin mistakenly tries to put it on, you're going to need to perform emergency alterations or find a substitute jacket. I've seen grooms whip out a stapler and staple the seam closed from the inside of the jacket, and I've seen sewing-kit-wielding mothers and grandmothers appear like magic to solve a hem dilemma. Think fast and solve the problem as best you can. If the women can solve their own alteration snafus with safety pins, iron-on hem webbing, and even duct tape, so can you.

One other option: switch jackets with a groomsman who's close to your size. He's not the man of the hour; he can have one sleeve longer than the other.

Take one final look in the mirror, you sharp-dressed man, and head off to impress your bride and your guests.

8

◇ ◇ ◇

Wedding Rings

YOUR WEDDING RINGS are more than just pricey pieces of jewelry—they're the tangible symbols of the vows you'll take on your wedding day. The circle of the wedding band means "eternity," and that symbol tells the world that you are part of an unbreakable duo. These rings stay with you day in and day out, so you'll need to be sure that you both choose a style of ring you can live with every day for the rest of your lives. Design is one thing, quality is another. What you're looking for is not only an attractive ring, but one of top quality, durability, and value. By that, I mean you want *the best* ring out there in your price range, and not an inferior ring that will turn your finger green or slice open the sides of your fingers with an attractive but lethal laser-cut design.

In this section, you'll delve into the world of wedding rings, using the knowledge you already mastered when you chose the engagement ring using the 4 C's (color, cut clarity, and carat) and your general shopping smarts. You'll learn about the new trends in wedding bands and ways to leave a sentimental mark on them forever, as well as a few pointers on how to get better rings for a better price.

What's Your Ring Style?

Check out your own ring finger right now. Go ahead and look. In just a short time, you're going to be sporting a band of gold (or platinum or silver), so you'll need to think about what style of ring you want to find a permanent home on your hand. Are you the traditional type, where it's classic and elegant all the way with a pure gold rounded-edge band? Understated. Not too flashy. Or are you into more modern designs, the same as you might find in art and architecture, where it's going to be dual-metals, an intricate laser-cut design—something to really catch the eye? Do you want Claddagh rings? Or a ring with a tiny embedded diamond chip for a little extra sparkle and the same claim to "diamonds are forever" that your bride has?

The good news for you is that men's wedding-band designs are more varied and plentiful than ever. A few decades ago, you'd have to look pretty hard to find something beyond the standard plain gold band. But now, ring designers are opening up great new worlds with fabulous metals, diamonds, and a variety of other gemstones that look great on the male hand. And not Liberace's hand, either. These manly rings are as smooth and streamlined as an Armani suit, and they allow today's man to exert his personal style.

Customized Circles

Custom-designing your own wedding band is hot now. For a comparable price to buying new, you or an artist friend can sketch out the shape, size, and design of your wished-for wedding band, and take it to a metalsmith or custom jeweler who will fashion it into your own one-of-a-kind ring. Check out jewelry-design experts near you, or go to a diamond center in a big city to scout out the details. Your bride can also custom-design her own ring at Web sites like www.bluenile.com and www.adiamondisforever.com, then take the printout and accompanying stone description to a custom jeweler. The do-it-yourself trend in rings is equal opportunity.

Before you take another step, let me help you define your personal style for that wedding band. Answer these questions now so that you can answer them when the sales attendant at your ring shop sits you down in front of millions of dollars' worth of jewelry and helps you narrow the field. This questionnaire is a time-saver, and it will make the process a lot easier:

1. *Do you prefer understated or eye-catching? Do you want the ring to stand out and people to notice it?*
2. *Do you want a simple metal band, or do you want some variation: diamonds or gemstones embedded, laser-cut design?*
3. *Do you prefer the color of silver or gold? How about a blend, say a silver edging to a gold ring or vice versa?*
4. *What color are your good watches?*
5. *Do you want a thin or thick band?* (Most men prefer to try on examples of both to see which looks better with the length and thickness of their fingers and hands. On some hands, the thinner band looks better, while the thicker ones look too overpowering.)

My best advice is to bite the bullet and flip through some of your fiancée's bridal magazines and check out men's wedding ring styles. This is a good Sunday-morning shared activity with your bride, so get breakfast in bed ready, make some coffee, and share this fun task with her as you *both* peruse the various ring

---

Are plain metal bands always less expensive than the ones with the fancy designs, cut-outs, and dual-type metals?

No, not always. You will find a variety of less expensive standard metal bands out there, but you can spend top dollar on a high-end traditional ring, a designer name, and top-grade platinum for your bands. So it's not always a rule that plain costs less, even though additional workmanship and detail to rings usually does add up to higher prices. As with all things wedding budget, you'll need to seek individual price deals and not limit yourself to always/never rules.

styles spotlighted in the glossy magazines. Jewelry Web sites are also a great tag-team Web-surfing session for both of you, so visit your (or her) favorite jewelry site and check out the offerings, bookmarking your favorite options. Print out your top choices and keep them for when you go live and in-person to the jewelry store

together. Again, your initial search is meant to acquaint you with the types of designs out there, as well as the appearance and shine factor of the metal varieties you'll have to choose from. You're narrowing your search.

Remove Ring Before Painting the House

One thing you absolutely must think about when checking out styles of wedding rings is the kind of wear and tear your rings are likely to receive every day. Grooms who work with their hands—such as doctors, chefs, masons, and athletes—should probably choose a ring with minimal detailing and smoother edges. Guys who work with chemicals or who spend time in chlorine-filled pools and hot tubs on a regular basis might look at rings in a "can this one take that kind of exposure?" way. You men don't often think about the durability of your jewelry the way women do, but you should. Will you choose a ring with a smooth edge and no grooves or with details that will constantly collect dirt? Will you make a practice of removing your ring during work? It may sound like a small detail, but, you won't want to spend a lot of time de-gunking your wedding ring, and I'm sure you don't want to provoke your future wife's constant shrills of "Why aren't you wearing your ring?!"

The Wedding Ring Primer

Once you have a ring style in mind (smooth versus detailed, silver versus gold, thin versus thicker), it's time to learn the basics of wedding bands. Knowing the difference between 24-karat gold and 18-karat gold, platinum and white gold is going to put you ahead of the game when it's time to slap on the smart consumer cap and take your credit card to the jewelry store. The more you know in the ring realm, the better your chances of selecting the finest ring possible at a reasonable price, and the better your odds of keeping up with a fast-talking ring salesperson before he sells you on something you don't want and can't afford.

Platinum

The first metal you're likely to hear about is platinum. Right now, platinum is the metal-of-choice in bands for its durability and shine, as it's the strongest of available ring metals and thus a better buy for everyday wear. Its popularity for wedding bands makes it one of the most expensive options, but I urge you to consider a platinum ring to be a wise investment. Going for cheaper metals just because they "look silvery" will almost certainly let you down in the long run when your "cheaper" bands get dented, diamond chips dislodge from faulty settings, and your finger develops a green tinge after a week's wearing. Platinum, by contrast, never tarnishes and is 100 percent hypoallergenic. So that makes buying it money well spent.

What to Look For

When you're looking at platinum rings, know that they are usually created from a blend of 95 percent platinum and 5 percent alloys of iridium or palladium. Look on your rings for the markings of 900 Pt, 950 Plat, or Plat.

For detailed information on shopping and caring for platinum jewelry, contact the Platinum Guild International, www.preciousplatinum.com, 949-760-8279.

18-Karat Gold

If platinum rings don't fit into your budget right now, you can get the same look and nearly the same durability by substituting 18-karat gold. White gold has the shiny, silvery look of platinum and is a very popular choice for wedding bands.

Traditional yellow gold is also up there on wish lists, since both types claim good durability and don't tarnish or rust.

So which is a better choice for your rings—24-karat gold, 18-karat gold, or 14-karat gold? Most couples guess the higher number, but did you know that 24-karat gold is actually *less ideal* than 14-karat? That's because 24-karat-gold is one of the most malleable metals out there. Bumps, dings, and dents are all more likely to mar a 24-karat-gold piece of jewelry. Remember: the higher the number, the softer the metal. In the ring creation process, designers incorporate strong alloys into the metal mixtures, bringing durability up the lower the numbers go.

What to Look For

Jewelers say that you're better off looking for 14- or 18-karat gold for wedding jewelry, rather than 24-karat. They will hold up better.

Sterling Silver

Sterling silver is another top choice for wedding bands, and it is probably the second best choice for couples who love the look of platinum but can't swing its high prices. Plus, if you're allergic to gold, silver may be the smartest choice. Pure-form silver is also among the softer and more malleable metals, so again alloys are often added to make it stronger. The average sterling silver ring is made of about 92.5 percent silver and 7.5 percent copper alloy, since copper doesn't affect the color of the silver while adding to its durability.

Just keep in mind, though, that silver and sterling silver rings are on the endangered species list when it comes to everyday damage from chemicals, cleansing products, chlorine and fluoride in tap water, pool water, and hot tub water. Silver jewelry can be damaged if you're not careful to avoid these kinds of oxidants, which can actually weaken your rings, dull their shine, and hurt their appearance in other ways. Even some acidic foods like lemon juice and tomato sauce can sometimes dull or damage silver jewelry. Bear these facts in mind if

What to Look For

When checking out sterling silver jewelry, check for official quality grading marks such as "sterling," "ster," and ".925."

you're leaning toward choosing silver. It's gorgeous and affordable, but it does require extra TLC in handling and maintenance.

Before you put this book down to watch some NASCAR or head to the driving range to shake off this frou-frou ring stuff, take into account that your ring doesn't have to be all shiny and sparkly. Hammered finishes are hot right now, and can give your ring that manly new-but-not-too-new look.

Ring Settings

Settings for diamonds and stones were probably more of a concern while you were choosing your fiancée's engagement ring, so you may have some background information already. But if you want wedding bands that feature precious stones, then settings move back onto your ring-shopping radar.

The setting that holds any stones can actually improve the sparkle of the diamond, emerald, ruby, or other rock you've selected for your bands. A great setting can lift the stone and allow the light to move through the facets, giving them that dazzling sparkle and perhaps even making the rock look bigger and more impressive. On the flip side, a less-than-optimal setting can make a real dazzler look flat. So you'll need to check out the possible settings for any diamonds or stones that will be a part of either of your wedding bands.

Here are the most common types of stone settings for any type of ring:

- *Bezel:* Stones are encircled and embedded in the ring by thin strips of the band's metal, whether gold, platinum, or silver.
- *Channel:* One of the most popular settings for wedding bands right now and probably the one your jeweler will show you first, the channel sets smaller stones in a straight line through the center of the band, secured in place by two raised metal strips on either side of the stones.
- *Cluster:* The cluster gathers a group of stones in the same manner as a floral bouquet, with one larger stone in the center. (Note: this one is more of an engagement ring style, so consider this if you plan to upgrade that engagement ring in the years to come!)

- *Invisible:* Gemstones are set in place very close together, with the binding metal fastener hidden underneath the stones.
- *Pave:* Like a paved road, the ring presents the stones in a carefully arranged flat pattern that gives more sparkle for the amount of stones that are there. Jewelers say this is a great way to make a more modest investment really shine.
- *Prong:* Like a clamp, tiny metal arms are tightened around the edges of the stone to hold it in place. Prong settings are usually reserved for engagement rings, to give that lift to diamonds.
- *Tension:* The stones are held tightly between two rings of metal, using the tension between them to secure the stones' position.

One of the hottest settings right now are stackables, which work well for women's wedding and engagement ring pairings. Rather than place one wedding band next to the engagement ring on her married hand, you'll provide two separate, diamond-set bands to serve as "sandwich" wedding bands surrounding her engagement ring. You may well want to take a look at this great modern styling for your bride.

And for you, the new square-shaped ring is hot. The inner band is round to fit your finger, but the outside edges are slightly squared with rounded edges for a really masculine, partly angled look. I particularly love the squared rings with a matte silver ridge running along the center, plus one or two diamond chips at the top. Very nice. And worth a look. Visit Scott Kay's Web site www.scottkay.com; these days he's pushing the most popular line of square rings for men.

Know Your Rocks

Embedding stones in wedding bands is another hot choice now, so don't be surprised if your bride wants even more diamonds in her wedding ring set. You, groom, can go for smooth and stoneless, or you can add some sparkle to your ring with tiny diamond chips. Guys' rings look great with tiny chips in either standard round or geometric shapes. When you're looking at stone-embedded men's rings, you might see oval stones, squares, starbursts, or other shapes, owing to the huge explosion in original design and style out there. Guys' rings are getting artsy, with embedded stones and laser-cut designs, or layers of different metals to get the best of both worlds in silver and gold. So look through the styles out there, and ask if you're a diamond guy as well.

The 4 C's: A Reminder

Sure, you've already read about a diamond's 4 C's: color, cut, clarity, and carats. Each category has gradings that qualify the ring according to these four most important characteristics of a good stone. A diamond grading report for each stone will list marks for the stone's individual qualities, and you'll use that information to make your choice. Here's how each stone gets its "pedigree": a gemologist inspects the diamond under a high-powered microscope and, using a precise system, assigns grading numbers or letters to the stone. The ranking of each category (color, cut, clarity, and carats) affects the price of the ring, depending on its proximity to perfection in each area.

What to Look For

Always ask to see the grading certificate and inspect the grading information for any stone you're considering. If there is no grading certificate, don't even look at that stone. A qualified stone will have its own "diploma."

Color: Diamonds come in colors ranging from pure white to deep yellow, and even in fabricated shades such as pink, lavender, and ice blue. The pure white ones, as they're called when they have almost no color, are the most valuable. Such perfect color makes it much more expensive. Colorless diamonds are given a grading of D through F, and the variations from there are indicated as follows: excellent, near-colorless G through J, yellowish K through M, and then Y through Z, which are more yellow and in a lower price range. You'll want to strike closer to the G range than the Y range, since very few brides want a diamond that looks like it's been steeped in coffee for a few years. Aim for the more colorless part of the grading range, and you'll find a better stone at a lower price. Your naked eye probably won't be able to detect the difference between a J and a K, but you'll be able to see a world of difference between that D and Z.

Cut: The cut of the diamond is of supreme importance, as the shapes and number of facets the stone is cut into determine its appearance, angles, and sparkle. The more facets (or flat planes) a ring has, the more its surfaces catch the light and the more sparkle the ring has. Jewelry experts say that the cut is the most impressive quality of any ring and should therefore be given the most thought. The most popular cuts are:

- *Princess:* A square design that can be either a true square, a rectangle, or a cushion-cut
- *Round:* Round, and the most popular choice right now, sometimes called "brilliant round"
- *Oval:* Makes a round look larger
- *Marquise:* Like a sideways eye
- *Lozenge:* Like a marquise cut, but with more pointed edges
- *Emerald:* More square
- *Pear:* Pear-shaped
- *Heart:* Heart-shaped
- *Asscher:* A revived Old-World style, this celebrity favorite is a sparkling square-cut with a high crown and a staggering 74 facets that draw light *into* the stone for more sparkle emanating through its layers. Also found in round, emerald-cut, octagonal shapes for a mix of timeless elegance with modern design. Visit www.royalasscher.com for a look at varieties and celebrity styles

Stone shapes are again more of a concern for the engagement ring, but I include the subject here as a reminder that you *do* have options when it comes to the shapes of any precious or semiprecious stones that you might want embedded in the rings for both you and her. Know that the gemstone field is packed when it comes to cuts of any precious stone, so explore your options.

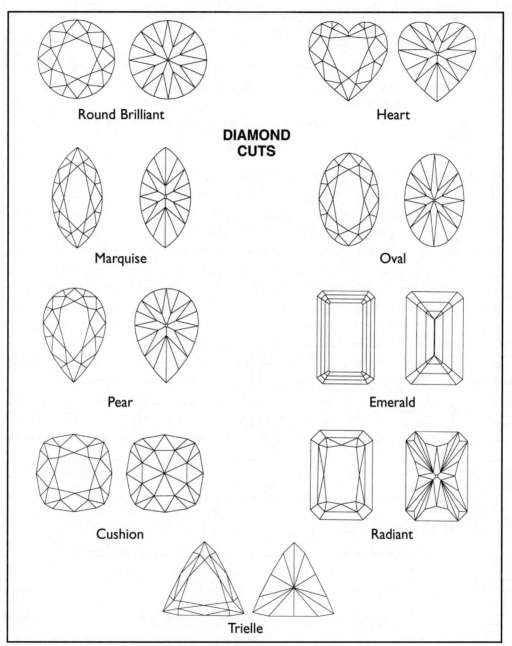

Round Brilliant

Heart

DIAMOND CUTS

Marquise

Oval

Pear

Emerald

Cushion

Radiant

Trielle

What to Look For

A stone's clarity is graded according to a universal scale: FI is perfect (and far more expensive); VS is "very slightly included"; SI is "slightly included"; and I or FI3 is imperfect. Inclusions and blemishes should be noted and mapped on the stone's certification papers, quantifying the effect they have on the stone's price.

Clarity: The clarity of a stone refers to how perfect it is throughout. In the world of precious stones, you're talking about a hunk of carbon that has come out of the earth as a raw diamond to be cut, polished, and shaped. Mother Nature isn't held to any standards, practices, or labor laws, so each of her designs comes out differently. Some stones might have spots of carbon remaining within. Other stones may sport minuscule cracks or fissures deep inside that you can't even see without the use of a jeweler's microscope or loupe. Regardless of whether you can see those cracks or spots, they do count when it comes to grading a stone for clarity. The more perfect stones are flawless, truly without any internal or external marks (called "inclusions" or "blemishes"). But you're going to pay through the nose for the most perfect of stones, if you can find one outside of a museum. Nearly all diamonds and stones have flaws, so look for those on the lower-end of the flaw-o-meter.

Since you're talking about tiny stones for you, you probably will have no problem accepting a stone that's somewhat less perfect. The price will be right, and the flaw not visible if you're not looking for it. For your bride's rings, though, choose a ring with the best clarity you can afford.

What to Look For

A full carat diamond sports a one-carat grading; anything less is called a light carat. And notice that when carat refers to stones it is spelled with a *c*; when referring to metals, karat is spelled with a *k*. Just FYI.

Birthstones by Month

Want to go symbolic and use your birthstones? Whether you use this information for your wedding bands or for a meaningful separate jewelry gift for your bride (or as a great wedding-day gift for one of her family members), here are the stones that match the months:

January: Garnet
February: Amethyst
March: Aquamarine
April: Diamond
May: Emerald
June: Pearl

July: Ruby
August: Peridot
September: Sapphire
October: Opal
November: Topaz
December: Blue topaz

Carats: The size of the diamond is dictated by its carat weight, with a carat weighing approximately one-fifth of a gram. Higher carat counts usually mean higher price tags, but the other 3 C's affect the pricing just as much. It all works together to add up to the obvious: the better the quality, the more you'll pay.

Going for Color

While diamonds are the most popular stones used in grooms' rings, you can also go for a hint of color by choosing gemstones with color. You might use the birthstones for you, your bride, and even your child or children if you have them. Some types to choose from are amethyst (purple), aquamarine (blue), citrine (yellow), emerald (green), garnet (red, oranges, purples), and ruby (red). Some gemstones are more expensive than others, but again the cost depends on the stone's grading and quality of cut.

Always remember to ask your jeweler about the gemstone's grading on the Moh's scale, or test of the stone's durability. You will find that most of the lighter-hued gemstones are less expensive than the brighter ones. Just price a ruby or an emerald next to a citrine to see the difference. Why the primary-color price bump?

In the course of preparing gemstones to be made into jewelry, the stones may be heat-treated to intensify their natural colors—a paler green may become deeper, for instance. This special heat treatment makes the stone more valuable, and therefore more expensive; a very important factor when you're looking at these stones. Be sure to inquire whether any stone you're considering has been heat treated. Such a procedure doesn't only increase the price of the stone, it increases certain risks for the stone in the future. A heat-treated ring can be less resilient to solid impacts, ring-cleaning chemicals, and even extreme temperature changes— so ask and get your answer before plunking down your cash.

Going Outside the Box

You might be the type of couple who prefers an heirloom ring, perhaps taking the stone from your grandmother's engagement ring and giving it to your bride in a new setting. Welcome to the brave new world of wedding-ring creation, where family sentiment remains in a shiny new package. Heirloom rings are popular right now. Resetting your mother's, your grandmother's, or her mother's or grandmother's, stones into a modern setting might be a great move for you in a budgetary *and* sentimental way.

Another move might be looking outside of established jewelry stores for your rings. I know, I told you to stick with the most reputable, longest-standing professionals out there, but you might want to try antique shops or estate sales to find a ring with a story. If you wish to go this alternate route, please be sure to deal only with established professionals, pay with credit cards, sign good contracts with return and refund clauses, and get your rings appraised and insured immediately. Here are some terms you should know in order to tell true antiques from vintage . . . terms *she'll* know about and be impressed you know too:

- ◆ Rings termed *antique* are more than one hundred years old. They're authentic, not just dirty, faded rings from the 1950s.
- ◆ Rings termed *vintage* have an antique look, might be of a style and design that is no longer produced, and are less than one hundred years old
- ◆ Rings termed *estate* are previously owned, have perhaps been sold at auction or on the private market, in shops or boutiques.
- ◆ Rings termed *costume* are made from imitation gemstones, which isn't always a bad thing. Back in the old days, very high-quality jewelry with fabulous detail and custom styling sometimes held fake gemstones. So you might find very valuable "fakes" selling for beaucoup bucks.

Politically Correct Stones

Yes, the PC crowd has struck again, this time at diamonds and other gemstones, and you might not be as miffed about this topic as you might be about the push to end reciting the Pledge of Allegiance in the classroom. News hounds have reported that underworld honchos and some terrorist brigades have financial stakes in the diamond trade. So that means that when you buy a diamond, the money might be going to a madman. Similarly, tribal wars raging in Africa and Asia can be funded by the trafficking and sale of diamonds and gemstones, with the citizens of those regions paying a high price while the warring continues. So if you are concerned about global politics, you might not want to buy a diamond that's been mined in a sociopolitical minefield.

One good way to avoid "conflict diamonds" is to shop only at reputable jewelers, who are less likely to buy street diamonds or gems from shady networks. If you deal through the Jewelers of America (www.jewelers.org, 800-223-0673), you can actually find out from a jeweler they recommend where your proposed diamond came from and whether it might be a conflict stone. At the time of this writing, I happily learned that Tiffany was investigating partnership in a new diamond mine in Canada.

Getting the Fit Just Right

When I asked several brand-new grooms how their rings felt on their hands, most said the rings were so comfortable, they didn't even know they had them on. Some complained of irritation from a rough edge, and said they'd soon be getting the ring refitted and for more comfortable wear. A few jokers came out with "It burns!" as a riff on their adjustment to marriage. Overall, these guys wanted their rings to feel like a part of their hand. No tightness, no cutting edges, no getting in the way.

What you're looking for in terms of fit is size and comfort. You might select a "comfort fit band," a style that isn't squared or angular-edged, but sports a rounder edge.

Choosing the right size is key. Be sure to get your ring finger measured by a professional with ring-sizing templates. These will be slid onto your finger to determine your correct ring size. Order true to your size for a snug pull over your knuckle but a secure fit on your hand. You want the ring to come off when you want it to and not when you don't want it to.

Individuals or Sets

So what happens when you're out ring-shopping with your bride, and she spots a gorgeous his-and-hers wedding-band set that will cost you less as a joint purchase . . . but you hate the design of the *his* ring in the set? Please, please, please don't give her the "Yes, dear." You're going to have to live with the ring you choose, so this is the time to speak up if she wants you to wear a way-too-flowery or way-too-intricate design. You *can* find separate, non-set wedding bands for less than a packaged set, so spend extra time looking through the store's selection. Plus, it might be convenient, but it's not a rule that you have to buy both of your wedding rings in the same store.

But you should shop in a reputable, high-quality jewelry store. Always shop at jewelry stores that have been in their present locations for a long time, and have a great reputation with their clients and referrals from your own family and friends. A great ring shop can help you tremendously with your ring selection, and can even help you select coordinating his and her rings that are *not* a boxed set, at a discount.

When you're checking out jewelry shops, you're looking for attentive service from salespeople who really know their stuff. You want to be treated with respect. You want your questions answered patiently and completely. And you want to feel comfortable with the person who will be selling you some of the most important things you'll ever buy in your life.

You'll want to be sure the store's stock is varied and displayed beautifully, that everything is clean and sparkly. You want the store to be in top shape, clean, orderly, and well lit. Look around. Do you see other couples shopping there? Do they appear to be well taken care of by the staff member assisting them?

During your first moments with the sales associate, is he or she only too happy to pull out the rings you'd like to see up close? The best ring consultants are very well aware that this decision is not easy, and that it might take you a while to make it. You won't be rushed or subjected to a hard sell. You're not going to get the "You'd better choose now, I have other people coming to look at that one" routine. The best shops I've visited are there to help you, not push you. Take all the time you need.

Top ring agents will point out markings on the bands to show you the tiny platinum stamp, and they'll let you view stones through their machines for a closer look at a chip's true design. This attention to detail will make ring shopping more enjoyable. You'll get documents on your rings, and you'll be informed of true prices, any sales, and the length of time it will take for your rings to come in. The sales associate will give you a read-through of the contract, answer any of your questions, and brief you on the next steps of appraising and insuring your rings. You'll get pamphlets on care and cleaning of your rings, maybe a free cleaning machine or solution, and possibly a gift for your patronage. The greatest ring shops really know how to do it, because if they get it right, if they really give you the royal treatment, you're going to come back for future birthday and anniversary gifts. That's another reason I always recommend that you ask friends and family for referrals to their favorite jewelers. A beautiful relationship can develop over the years.

What About Department Stores?

Don't count out department store jewelry counters for your wedding bands. You'll sometimes find great deals on quality rings, provided you remember to check for grading certificates and proof of quality. Especially during big-time jewelry sale seasons, you could net great rings at a great price. One couple I know bought their rings at a local Costco's jewelry counter. They found beautiful rings in high-quality 14-karat gold, at a price that was $200 lower than any they found in jewelry stores. As smart consumers, they had the rings appraised and insured immediately, and they boasted about their great find.

What to Watch For

If you must shop for wedding bands over the Internet, please keep the following smart e-consumer rules in mind:

- Know your metals and stones inside and out. With Internet shopping, you probably won't have a seasoned pro at your side to help you sort out the best from the worst.
- Use the same smart shopping rules you'd use for any jewelry purchase.
- Choose a Web site that has a legitimate street address, not just a web address. This is very important so that you know where to return your merchandise . . . or where to serve the papers if you have to take them to court for a refund.
- Shop only through a Web site that provides a 100 percent guaranteed return and refund policy.
- Print out the fully itemized order sheet that spells out the particulars of the ring you've ordered.
- Get and print out an independent grading report on any diamonds or stones to be used in your ring.
- Use your credit card to secure your purchase. Credit card purchases can be tracked and protected for your safety.
- Don't use a debit card for this purchase, since many debit cards don't provide the kind of protection credit cards do.
- Use a credit card that has a points or reward program. This is going to be a big purchase, so you might as well get a little kickback.
- Only shop on sites that are guaranteed secure, with that little lock in the bottom corner. If your computer's security system says this isn't a secure site, go elsewhere
- Check your order for a guaranteed date of delivery. Again, if it doesn't give you some range, go elsewhere.
- Check the Better Business Bureau at www.bbbonline.org to see whether a site has been in any trouble, and use that information as only a portion of your site research. Just because something is not listed on BBB doesn't automatically make it clean.
- Ask friends for referrals to jewelry Web sites they've used and trust.

Internet Ring Shopping

You can shop for rings over the Internet, but be sure you're shopping at a reputable, well-known site with a solid track record, top-notch security, and a guaranteed return policy. There is so much fraud on the Internet that some people are skittish about shopping for such an important item on the Web. But if you're a savvy online shopper, you might find just the right product at a completely reliable source. Be sure the site has a street address, and try to stick with established companies like Bloomingdales, Macy's, Tiffany, Ross Simons, and others. Use the Better Business Bureau's online watchdog site at www.bbbonline.org to check up on sites, and employ your best judgment.

Be aware that if you shop online, you'll deprive yourselves of that fun trip to the jewelry store. Check with your bride before you make an online purchase to see if she has her heart set on in-person shopping. She might not be dreaming about having your wedding bands brought to you by the UPS man.

Making Your Mark

Having a little something special engraved inside your wedding bands adds an extra dose of sentiment to them. You might choose to surprise your bride by having the jeweler sketch in an "I Love You" or "Forever" or your wedding date inside her band, or you can go original with something like the following:

- *Always Faithful*
- *Love Forever*
- *Je t'aime* (or "I Love You" in any language)
- *I Adore You*
- *My Wife, My Friend*

- *Walk with Me Forever*
- Her nickname
- The date you met
- The date you proposed
- The city where you proposed
- The title of "your song"

One groom from California wrote in to share his ring-engraving story with me. He had the word *Lucky* engraved on his bride's ring. When she looked puzzled, he told her he chose that word because *she* was lucky to have *him*. After he got his playful punch in the arm, he confided that he chose that word because he felt like the luckiest man on earth to have her for his bride. Just that one word said it all, and the bride will always remember how he joked his way into a very romantic expression.

Engraving will be the least of your ring expenses, but you should know that jewelers charge by the letter. You choose the font from the engraver's sample list, triple-check the spelling and the accuracy of the wording or numbers you use (get that date you met right—she will know it by heart!), and place your order in writing with a solid contract and specific date of delivery. Pay by credit card and keep the receipt in a safe place. This may be a sentimental move, but it's also a business deal. So protect yourself.

Appraisals

Your first step after buying rings that feature diamonds and precious stones should be to get them appraised by a qualified jeweler. Especially in order to insure them (which is always a good move), you'll need to have on record exactly what they are worth. It's smart practice to go to a shop other than the one where you bought the rings to ensure objectivity and truth in assessing their value. Get an appraisal certificate and hang on to it for any future legal needs. Beyond the written value of the ring, a full appraisal will include a top-quality digital close-up photograph, the exact and scientific dimensions and grading of the stones, a description of the mount style, and a complete inventory of the stones' inclusions or blemishes, including a mapped template of these flaws. You'll need all this information to protect your ring investments for the future, so be sure to obtain your appraisal from a reputable jeweler.

Insurance

You read earlier about wedding insurance and other legalities, and insuring your engagement and wedding rings is another smart move. You might find that your homeowner's policy already includes a clause or two on protecting fine jewelry, but you should nevertheless check the fine print. Some policies protect

What to Watch For

Whenever you're assessing insurance policies or riders, read the fine print and ask plenty of questions. Even really creative, slightly neurotic questions, since those are the ones that are most likely to match up to the dangers lurking in real life. For instance, Does this policy cover your rings only if they're lost within the walls of your home, or are you covered if your rings are stolen on vacation? What about if *you* lose the ring in the sand during a family vacation or your band slips down the drain? Does your policy cover your rings if they're damaged in any way, or if one of the smaller stones falls out? Get specific, and ask these questions. You can do no better job of protecting these very valuable investments than insuring them against all possible scenarios.

jewelry only up to a rather low ceiling. If you spent $3,000 on your rings (which is pretty easy to do when you're talking one engagement ring and two wedding rings), what good does your policy do you if it only protects up to $500 or $1,000 worth of jewelry? If your policy contains a low ceiling for value, you'll certainly want to look into purchasing a separate rider that will cover the cost of your new rings. Talk to your insurance agent, and acquire the right additional coverage.

Some terms to know when you're looking at insurance for your rings (and her wedding day jewelry):

- A *blanket policy* will cover your rings within a group that includes other fine jewelry and valuables in your possession, setting a dollar limit for the value of each item you own.
- A *replacement policy* will cover the cost of buying a new ring of the same stated value, provided you meet the qualifications within the insurance policy's terms (which can get very involved).
- A *rider* is an extension to your existing policy. It's an extra patch of insurance you can buy for new items and conditions, or to increase the dollar value of your coverage.

So what happens if there's no coverage for jewelry under your existing plan, and your insurance agency has no provisions for fine jewels and important heirlooms? You'll need to research independent jewelry insurance companies for a separate policy. It's just an additional plan for additional cost, but it will be worth the steps to get it. Ask your married friends or jewelry-happy relatives who their insurers are. You can choose from several levels of coverage, at several levels of expense, depending on your needs.

It's smart to keep your appraisal certificate, insurance plans, and photographs of yourselves with your rings (to further prove ownership) in a bank safety deposit box or other fireproof box. These documents are your protection for these investments, and you'll be happy to have them when and if the unexpected comes to pass. Treat these papers like fine jewels, since they may become every bit as valuable as the stones in your rings.

There's Always Time to Upgrade Later

Your wallet might be screaming right now, and the idea of spending yet another couple of hundred (if not thousand) dollars on wedding rings is just plain painful. You might know that your bride would love a more diamond-bedecked wedding band, but she understands your current budget limitations. If the two of you are paying for your own wedding, as is often the case these days, it's understandable that you might not be able to shell out huge sums for the most incredible rings.

But there is a glimmer of hope. . . .

Upgrading your wedding bands (and even her engagement ring) down the road is becoming a hot trend. Couples who were in their lean years when they married and who chose modest bands are now improving their rings for their first, fifth, tenth, or twentieth wedding anniversaries. Later on, once you're even more set in your careers, once those college loans are all paid off, and once you have money in the bank, you can join the ranks of couples who are taking in their rings for a little servicing. Some get better-quality diamonds embedded where their old, okay stones once were (saving the original stone, of course, and having it made into a pendant for the sentimentality of its use on the wedding day). Or they're having their original stones reset into better-quality platinum bands since those high platinum prices have become within reach.

You might want to get a different setting for her engagement ring, or get her a new platinum bridge to add a layer of sparkle to her ring ensemble. It might be time to switch her from a Tiffany prong setting to that lower-set cathedrale setting, so that she's not always snagging her diamond on her stockings, or you might wish to leave a place for your future kids' birthstones on a separate band that coordinates with her wedding band and engagement ring. The sky's the limit, so know now that this wedding ring you're getting doesn't have to be the final version. You can upgrade it and adjust it as the years go by.

The ring is the thing for the ceremony, and the rings stay on your hands forever. The rings are among your most important purchases. So choose wisely and choose together.

9

◇ ◇ ◇

Building a Beautiful Ceremony

YOUR CEREMONY is the most important element of the wedding day, yet it often gets downplayed in favor of the more exciting parts of wedding planning, like the reception menu, the entertainment, the flowers, and the cake. Compared to the importance of your marriage ritual, those things *mean* very little. Here I'd like to help you both start to build your ceremony, the center of your day and the big turning point in your lives.

Before we start, I want you to think about the power of your commitment to one another. I want you to think about how important the words you speak will be. These are your promises to each other, the words you'll both remember forever, and the foundation of your partnership. You proposed to her for a reason: You wanted her to become your wife and share her life with you. You didn't take that step lightly, and you shouldn't take the ceremony lightly either. So read on to start mapping out everything about your ceremony—the menu and cake can wait!

The First Steps

Your very first steps in planning your ceremony are deciding the where and when. Most couples can't even start planning their reception until they've found a church, synagogue, or other location with a day open and an officiant willing to marry them. It may sound simple, but let me assure you . . . especially in peak wedding months (May through August), most churches and synagogues are fully booked. There are only so many weekends in each month, and thousands of marrying couples are out there right now trying to schedule their time slots. So work on this as early as humanly possible. Some couples book two years in advance just to reserve their own church. From availability to institutional red tape, you might be surprised at how tricky the process of setting your reception foundation can be.

Finding the Place

For you there might be no question: You'll marry in the church or synagogue you've attended all your life. If you don't have strong ties to any one house of worship, you might choose to seek out another house of worship in your or her faith. If neither of you is practicing your faith, you might choose to hold your ceremony *outside* of a house of worship, such as marrying at the hotel where your reception will be, or in a grassy field, on the beach, at home in your yard, and so on. In fact, you can marry just about anywhere.

If you do wish to go the church or synagogue route, you'll need to call the house of worship to inquire about available days and times. But be warned: Many houses of worship have strict rules about who they will and won't marry, and they won't just marry anyone who calls on the phone to book a reservation. You're not setting up a tee time here, and the church may first want to interview you. Some churches won't marry you if you're not a dues-paying parishioner. Some couples go through a red-tape jungle in this area. Churches may not recognize them as members, even if they've attended every Sunday since they were four, if they never signed the church's roster of members.

When you are interviewed, you'll be informed of their requirements, such as classes you have to take. You might be asked to fill out a lengthy questionnaire, complete with essay questions and a psychological assessment of your backgrounds and future plans. Marrying people isn't taken lightly by these institutions, and they want to make sure they're guiding you their way. The assessment process can be very involved, or it might entail only one quick meeting in the officiant's office.

Be Aware!

Be sure when you're visiting churches and meeting with officiants that you take along any needed paperwork: divorce papers if you've been married before, annulment papers that have been granted by the church to dissolve any former marriage you had, even the death certificate of your deceased spouse. Houses of worship require this information in print before they'll agree to perform your wedding.

And now for the more enjoyable part: Visiting potential ceremony locations to determine how they look and feel to you. All red tape aside, you're also looking at the house of worship, hotel ballroom, grassy field, or your backyard with an eye for appearance. Does the setting match your wishes? Do you like the grand, cavernous, masterful architecture of the church downtown? Or is that gorgeous building way too big and grandiose for your small guest list?

Is that hotel ballroom ripe for great decorating, a canopy, atmospheric lighting, and flowers everywhere? Can you see yourselves marrying underneath a trellis in your backyard? You have to be able to picture it and see if you can make it happen.

What you're looking for is the attractiveness of the site and that it matches what you both envision for your day. Then you'll look at the more functional aspects of the site. Is it big enough to fit your guest list? Is there parking, or will your guests have to find their own parking on a city street? Are there restrooms? Is there a separate room where you or your bride can get dressed for the wedding on-site? How about air-conditioning? Is the place cooled, or will you have to bring in fans? Will the site be decorated already, such as a poinsettia-filled church

Unique Places to Marry

Couples today might prefer to hold their wedding somewhere other than a conventional house of worship. There can be many reasons ranging from a distancing from the church or even not being able to get permission from an officiant, a lack of openings in the churches they like, or just a wish to create their ceremonies their way rather than as prescribed by an establishment's rules and regulations. If this sounds like you, consider the following list of great secular places that more and more modern couples are choosing for their ceremony locations:

- Wineries
- Hotel ballrooms
- Terraces overlooking the beach
- Bluffs right on the beach
- Arboretums and botanical gardens
- Lighthouses
- Boats

- Backyards
- Scenic view areas with vistas of cities or mountains in the distance
- Museums
- Art galleries
- Lawns of historical estates

These places not only exist out there for your consideration; many welcome weddings. Being outside of the bridal box, and not specializing in weddings, their prices might even be lower, and you can't beat holding your wedding in an original place, rather than the same church where everyone you know got married. So consider this list, and check out other unique ideas of your own.

during the weeks before the Christmas holiday? These are some of the questions you'll have to ask of the site manager or officiant.

Take a walk through your site and envision what you can bring in that's not already there. For instance, if you're building your own site outside of a church, think about the size of tent you might want, the number of chairs you'll have to rent for your guests, any pathways you'll need to clear and prepare. Think about floral décor and lighting for an outside wedding in the dusk hours. Then think about renting restroom trailers for your guests' use, if that will be necessary. These extra expenses to make a ceremony site out of a plain landscape can get pricey, so consider the expense of building your own ceremony location from the ground up. This isn't meant to scare you away from the idea—just research the added expense for this very beautiful and personalized approach to setting up your location.

Once you've toured several locations, narrow the field: Consider the extra work and expense involved in each, and choose the one that meets all of your needs *and feels right to you*. Many couples know they've found the right location because they feel comfortable there and can see themselves getting married right at that spot.

Open Your Wallet

One issue that is likely to arise is the site-use fee, which you'll have to fork over to use any site from a church to a synagogue, a historical home or garden, or an arboretum. It might be nominal, such as a small church's requested donation of $50, or it might be astronomical, such as a well-known botanical garden's reservation fee of $10,000 or more (for use of the site after the establishment has been closed to the public, overtime use of their staff, security, parking attendants, and so on). So be sure to ask about this fee before you lock into any deal.

School Is in Session

Some houses of worship require you to attend premarital classes, workshops, and even overnight retreats. The purpose of these classes is to prepare you for a lifetime together. Houses of worship fully intend to marry you for life, so they make it a rule to get you communicating about your future marriage and how you plan to raise your children (hopefully in the faith in which you're marrying). These can be one- to three-day courses, or even more time-consuming six-weekend stints. You'll attend seminars, spend time talking alone or in groups, write journals, answer questionnaires, take quizzes, and open up the floor for the serious conversations that should precede any wedding.

Decide whether you're willing to participate, and perhaps even more important if you have the time and ability to attend if your house of worship requires such classes. In this mobile society, where you might live on one coast and marry on another to be back in your old hometown, how will you both get to that location six weekends in a row to attend classes? Perhaps your church will allow you to attend classes near you and just bring your "diploma" along as proof of your completion of the course. Or you might plan to fly in a week before your wedding to attend a two-day seminar. This is one of the red-tape issues I mentioned earlier: Required courses can present logistical challenges in your schedule, so be sure to consider the time and travel requirements.

Interfaith Weddings

It's common these days to find couples of differing faiths joining together in a ceremony that blends and incorporates *both* of their religions. If this is the case with you, you'll find yourself perhaps working with two different officiants who will guide you through the task of mixing and melding the various rituals and wordings of both your faiths in one all-inclusive ceremony.

The big work here may be finding an interfaith officiant, or one from each of your faiths who will agree to perform a dual-religion ceremony. It takes a bit of research, some extra phone calls, and a few meetings to put this package together, and you'll all work together to select the elements you want to include. Keep in mind that this task could have you learning even more about your faith, her faith, and the faith of your families. As uniting as religion can be to a couple, it's very important to many brides and grooms to explore each other's beliefs before marriage—and that process often intensifies when a wedding is in sight.

A larger issue than that for some couples is the intense feeling that comes from family members who *insist* that you hold to *their* most cherished beliefs in *your* ceremony. I've been told by many wedding coordinators and officiants that all-out brawls have erupted in families where parents, even grandparents, take it as a personal affront if the wedding couple isn't planning their ceremony by the Book. Grandma is giving death looks to the bride's mother for even suggesting that you not have a high mass. Families can get in your face over this issue, and you might have to call in some backup. Officiants often have to counsel not just the bride and groom but their entire extended families when the issue is interfaith blending.

If your wedding will be interfaith, do yourselves a favor and sketch out the elements of the ceremony as a team together with your officiant. When you bring in too many "experts" from the outside, planning can get out of hand. Yes, it's important to honor your heritage and your family's wishes, but not at the expense of what the *two* of you believe.

Read up on religious marriage rituals, ask other interfaith couples how they blended their beliefs and the elements of their weddings, and custom-blend your own ceremony. That applies as well if you'll incorporate ethnic rituals, such as wearing a crown of olive leaves, jumping a broom, circling the altar three times, or using cultural music or readings. It's always a wonderful thing to bring your heritage into your ceremony. Doing so makes for an event as unique as you are, gives your guests a fresh look into your lives, and can make your ceremony more colorful and memorable.

Think about what you want to bring into the mix. Talk with family elders and research your ethnic background if you don't know much about it. You might want to check out relevant Web sites dedicated to the preservation of cultural practices. Again, this delving into your own background can be bonding for you and for your new bride. It might add an extra element of richness to your marriage if you decide right now to get more in touch with your heritage and make it a greater part of your life.

Writing Your Vows

So what are you going to say? Will you recite the tried-and-true traditional wedding vows of "love, honor, and cherish until we are parted by death" or do you want to get more poetic (or less poetic)? Do you want to stay away from anything too cheesy ("You are my everything, my soul mate, my compass, my North Star!") and state more plainly that she's the woman you have loved and will always love, the woman you'll be faithful to and respect and share the road ahead with? Your options are wide open, as it's become the norm for couples to at least play with the traditional vows they're handed by an officiant. This is your ceremony, after all, and during it you'll probably speak the most important words of your lives.

Need some inspiration? Here are a few brainstorming questions. Have a beer, sit down with pen and paper, and sketch out your thoughts:

1. *How did you feel the first time you saw your fiancée?*
2. *When did you know she was The One for you?*
3. *What are the things you really love about her?*
4. *Were there any funny moments in the start of your relationship that still make you smile when you think about them?*
5. *What does she bring to your life?*
6. *What do you want to bring to her life now and in the future?*
7. *What most excites you about your future together?*
8. *What does marriage mean to you?*
9. *How has she made your life better (or you a better man)?*
10. *Do you love her more each day?*

When writing your vows, remember to keep them short and to the point. You're probably going to feel pressured and nervous on the wedding day, so you'll be grateful that you haven't mapped out a long speech to memorize and deliver. When it comes to the big moment, brevity is best, wit is welcome, and emotions *will* run high.

So now we get to the big issue: *What if I cry when I see her?* So many grooms express this concern to me and to their friends. They're men. They don't want to cry in front of their buddies. But I'll tell you, it's perfectly fine if you pump out a tear or two when you see your bride for the first time in her wedding gown. I don't mean sobbing like a kindergartner on the first day of school or your bride when she watches *Beaches*. But crying is a sign of having a full heart and *not* a sign of weakness. Real men do cry. So don't worry about it.

Rehearse your vows either in private or with your bride, and keep that index card in a safe place. Be sure you or your best man takes it along to the wedding,

What to Watch For

Real men have also been known to pass out at the altar. Some common reasons for this are extreme heat, dehydration, being hung over (you'd better not be!), shallow breathing while nervous, or locking your knees as you're standing there. You could be one of those guys you see on "America's Funniest Home Videos," at first swaying, looking spaced out, and then falling over like a redwood with your hands still clasped in front of you. It happens. To prevent yourself from taking a dive when you should be saying "I Do," remember to breathe, unlock your knees, and be hydrated and not still drunk from the night before, and you should be fine.

so that you have it on hand and don't have to stammer through the vows as you try to "wing it." One great idea now commonly practiced by today's brides and grooms is to have the vows printed in the wedding program or on a separate sheet of parchment paper. Your guests might not be able to hear you too clearly during the ceremony, and they'll be glad to be able to share your vows. In addition, it makes a great keepsake for the future.

Put It to Music

Building your ceremony also includes choosing the ideal music from start to finish. Music is usually played while your guests are arriving and during the processional (when the bride and bridal party walk toward you down the aisle). There may be special songs during the ceremony or during mass, as well as during the recessional (when you and your new wife lead back up the aisle after your I Do's). Classical music is among the top choices, with gospel, classics, and organ hymns also up there on the list.

Consider whether you want to use the church organist and choir to play your favorite songs, or if you'd like to hire an elegant harpist, flutist, pianist, or guitarist. A professional vocalist or opera singer can also be auditioned and hired to sing during your ceremony. From wedding favorites like "The Four Seasons" by Vivaldi to Beethoven's "Ode to Joy," traditional wedding music is the norm, but you can personalize your ceremony with newer songs, romantic classics like "At Last" by Etta James for a more secular wedding, or even a fun party song as you walk back up the aisle.

Flip through your CD collection, borrow classical music CDs from family, friends, or the library, download some songs from classical music sites or even Amazon, and ask recently married friends for suggestions on the songs they used and loved. But remember, this isn't a concert. Keep your selection to four or five pieces for the processional, one or two pieces during the ceremony, and one or two during the recessional. More than that can make the ceremony go on too long—especially if you're marrying on a hot day and people are sweltering. Short and sweet works best.

Readings

During the ceremony, you and your bride might choose to incorporate some readings, spoken-word performances, passages from your favorite poems, lines from Scripture, or original writings that you have created. An honored friend or relative might be asked to step up to the microphone to recite your readings, adding extra meaning and sentiment to your day. Among these meaningful readings might be a poem you both feel speaks exactly of your love for each other, a religious passage of importance to you, or even selections from letters you wrote to each other during your courtship (but without the risqué parts!). I especially love this last idea, since it gives the ceremony a uniquely personal touch.

Special Moments

In this age of personalizing ceremonies, you might choose from any of the following popular "special moments" in a wedding ceremony. Some you've seen before at other weddings, and some might spark a completely original idea:

- *Lighting a unity candle*: In most instances, the mothers of the bride and groom will step forward as part of the ceremony to light two taper candles symbolizing the light and life of your separate families. Then, later in the ceremony, after you've taken your vows, the two of you will step forward and use these individual candles to jointly light one larger, decorative candle to symbolize the light and life of your new blended family.

- *Lighting a memory candle*: If one or both of you have lost a family member, such as a parent, a sibling, a grandparent, or even several relatives, you might choose to start your ceremony with the lighting of a memory candle. This decorative single pillar candle will symbolize the spiritual presence of your loved ones.

- *Displaying portraits*: To honor the memory of a departed family member or friend, you might wish to display a framed portrait of that person. You can have a small altar or pedestal set up in a discreet corner of the ceremony site, with the picture, plus flowers and candles to surround it.

- *Building a bouquet*: Your parents and close family members might be invited to your altar to place into a crystal vase one single rose stem with some greenery. As each member of your family does so, a gorgeous bouquet begins to take shape. You and your bride then place the last two roses to complete the arrangement, and you'll save and dry that bouquet as a keepsake.

- *Bread, wine, and salt*: Some cultures incorporate food and spice items that symbolize wealth, fertility, and a long life together. So you might wish to use an ethnic ritual involving the presentation of food for its deep and rich meaning.

- *Play a song*: Surprise your parents, or the bride, by having a musician or vocalist play a meaningful song that you're dedicating to them. This type of special musical surprise and dedicated song is not just for the reception party—doing it now makes it a tribute to your family, or to your bride.

- *Put on a show*: Another planned or surprise display might be hiring bag-pipers, Native American drummers, trumpeters, a choir, or other specialty performers to begin or end your ceremony in an unforgettable way.

- *End it in style*: You might wish to release doves or butterflies after your vows are taken and your marriage sealed with a kiss. Other happy endings might include having the church bells or carillon echo a celebratory song as you walk down the aisle. A nighttime wedding might have your guests lighting sparklers (with safety in mind, of course) to light your way, or you might arrange to have fireworks blast off at just the moment you kiss. (Be sure fireworks are legal, acquired with permits, and under the management of a professional fireworks company. Please don't try this on your own!)

Programs

Printed programs let your guests know what's going on, who's who, and—perhaps most important on those hot summer days—how much of the ceremony is remaining. These pretty handouts are something you can make on your home computer, using quality parchment or glossy brochure paper, great graphics, and perhaps a digital picture of the two of you. You'll create the wording for each page of your program together, following either a standard program model or having some fun and getting really creative with an original design. Here are the parts:

- *The front cover*: announces your names, the wedding date, and perhaps the place where you're marrying. You could go with graphics or with that great picture of you both.
- *The first page*: lists the "who's who" of your bridal party, naming everyone by their roles and full names, including your parents and perhaps grandparents, any honored speakers, musical performers, the officiant, and others you wish to have recognized.
- *The second page*: outlines the steps of the ceremony, so everyone can follow along. You'll list the names of the songs performed during the arrival time, the advent of the processional, the readings, the songs during the ceremony, the reading of the vows, the exchanging of the rings, plus anything else you've arranged for the ceremony itself. Guests love being able to follow the "acts" like in a Broadway play program.
- *The third page or back cover (if folded)*: might hold a personal message of gratitude and love for your families, with thanks for helping bring your wedding together, or a copy of your vows. You might also wish to print your new home address and phone number for guests to have right away.

You can choose textured paper, colored paper, vellum-covered single-page programs—anything from the world of decorative paper and print styles. You can play with fonts, try out different graphics and borders, even edit your pictures to make you both look better. This is a job that many grooms love to volunteer for. They get to play with the computer, create an organized and attractive program, and get a *lot* of credit for helping with something that's relatively easy to do.

Time-Saver

Instead of printing out two hundred programs on your home computer, take one finished, perfected, and *spell-checked* copy (get everyone's names right, because this is a permanent record!) to a copy shop like Kinko's, OfficeMax, or Staples for flawless duplication and perhaps even collating and binding. Most couples accept the expense for the time it saves, and the high quality of the reproductions and fasteners.

What the Guests Will Throw at You

Just a quick mention about the birdseed, flower petals, and other things you might supply your guests with to toss at you as you triumphantly exit the ceremony site. Keep in mind that most sites have *rules* about these things (as they do for many other things, like taking pictures in churches) so you'll have to get permission for any post-ceremony toss-its you have in mind. Overall, rice is frowned upon as it poses a health hazard for birds who might clean up after you, and some sites will actually charge you for sweeping up your rose petals from the church steps before the next wedding rolls in. Smart couples are avoiding the mess (and the birdseed that goes down the front of the bride's dress) by having guests blow bubbles, ring bells, light sparklers or candles for nighttime exits, or even just sing a chosen song as the bride and groom race by. So consider the options for this little part of your ceremony's end, and remember that birdseed pouches usually need to be assembled and tagged with a little personalized note, whereas bubble bottles come ready as is. Just apply a computer-made circular label to the bottle, and you're good to go.

A Final Word About Your Ceremony

The ceremony is the start of your big day, so remember to give the bride a little something special. When you see her, tell her how beautiful she looks. Tell her you love her. She'll remember that always, and it might also help put her jangling nerves to rest. Take a moment to shake your dad's hand, kiss your mom, and similarly greet your new in-laws. Your dad will love that little wink you give to him when the music swells at the start of the processional, and your bride will be looking for signs of your happiness as she approaches you. Stay conscious of these *personal moments* at this important time, and remember to connect individually with everyone that's most important to you. Your bride might not remember years down the road which types of flowers were in her bouquet, but she's going to remember the look on your face forever. So give her the best memory possible, and be conscious enough to take memories for yourself as you really notice how proud your parents look and how happy your bride is that she's chosen *you* to spend her life with. I promise you, it's something you won't want to miss.

10

◇ ◇ ◇

Building Your Reception

LIKE YOUR CEREMONY, your reception must be built from the ground up. Here is where the bride, her parents, your parents, and everyone else can come at you with their images of the dream reception—a sea of flowers, crystal chandeliers, a glass-enclosed atrium where you can see the stars at night, Wolfgang Puck making little gold-leafed statuettes out of chocolate for everyone. No, wait. That's the banquet for the Oscars . . . but your troops can get the same starry-eyed visions for a five-star celebration—and it might be all on your dime. That's why you and your bride need to sit down right now and sketch out what *you* want for your reception.

What's Your Style

Again, are you thinking full formal dinner dance or something a little less stuffy? Cocktail-hour receptions are now very popular. These are an extended version of the usual prereception cocktail hour, with music playing in the background as the traditional cocktail hour goes on for three, four, or five hours. Food stations are scattered throughout the room, the bar is set up in one corner, and everyone mingles while they snack through a range of exotic and exciting menu options.

Avoiding that sit-down dinner could stretch the average budget to provide plenty of good culinary choices while making the reception unique for the guests. Plus, some guests much prefer those bacon-wrapped scallops, taquitos, phyllo squares, and pasta and carving stations over the same old ho-hum chicken and beef dishes with over-steamed veggies that are served at formal dinners.

Add to this unique reception style the fact that the southern tradition of *wandering* receptions is spreading throughout the country. At these original celebrations, guests go to one area (like an outdoor terrace) for king crab legs, shrimp cocktail, clams on the half shell, and other seafood snacks; they go to a separate room for fondue; and then go to another area for something else. Each "stop" along the way has a theme, which allows you to change the environment along with the menu. You're giving your guests four or five new mini-parties to look forward to, and this setup can make the most of a hotel's or estate's grounds and gardens.

Another option is the dessert-and-champagne reception. This takes place at night—eight P.M. or later—and guests gather in an elegant setting to enjoy fine champagne, coffee, espresso, cappuccino, after-dinner drinks, your cake and a range of pastries, mousse, pies, tarts, and chocolate-covered strawberries. No dry chicken here! It's all late-night indulgence and a sweet twist to the traditional reception. And yes, this style is also deceptively budget-friendly as well as being refined. Your guests won't know you're spending half what you would have spent on a full-blown five-course meal!

Or you could have a morning-hour brunch reception. Most popular on Saturdays and Sundays at about eleven A.M., the brunch reception makes the most of a daytime celebration—giving your guests a walk through a brunch buffet line with both breakfast and luncheon menu items: from crème brûlée waffles to Eggs Benedict, expertly presented and artistic fruit salads, ham and prime rib carving stations, and a wide array of mini-desserts and literally dozens of other dishes to choose from (not to mention the *free* champagne, mimosas, and bellinis). This kind of reception is likely to be different from the others your guests have been to, and it's easy on the wallet. Select the same exact menu for a late-afternoon or evening wedding, and you'll pay thousands of dollars more. The brunches I've seen are incredible. Pianists are playing. Tuxedoed maître d's treat you like royalty, the sun is shining, and guests can eat on outdoor terraces. The brunch is *the* hot reception trend for couples who want to go "different" in style but not sacrifice indulgence.

Of course, you can also choose a beach or backyard reception, clambake style, barbecue style, or formal-style. Outdoor settings can be arranged to suit every level of decorum, and they feature great scenery.

Want to celebrate on a boat? Can do. A private yacht? Just call the captain. Anything can be done for the reception style that's most *you*.

Location

Okay, now you have a handle on what kind of reception you want. You've thought about it from the very beginning, you've gone deeper into it now, so you know what you're looking for. All you need to do is find the place.

Think about places you've attended other weddings, anniversary parties, bar mitzvahs, First Communion parties . . . all those hotel ballrooms and party rooms, country clubs, private estates, private homes. See if there's anyplace you've been that would work for you. The best predictor of future happiness is past performance, so think about a location that really impressed you and add it to your list.

Now go ahead and ask friends, family members, colleagues, and others if they've been to any parties at places that might work for you. One smart move is to consider hiring a professional to help you find the best place. A wedding coordinator or a professional site scout can download a ton of information on resorts, restaurants, brunches, parks, botanical gardens, seaside banquet halls, and other places you might not be aware of. You can hire these experts just for the task of scoping out the best places in your area, or in your destination. I spoke with site scout Sarah Stitham of Charmed Places in Olivebridge, New York, for instance. Her company finds charming, rustic, or rambling resorts and mountainous overlooks in the Hudson Valley, the Adirondacks, and other New York–centric places for couples who want to get out of the city and into the country. She's hooked up brides and grooms with their own rented villas and ski resorts, or converted old barns and campyards into something right out of Shakespeare, giving her clients a completely personalized setting they'd never know about without her help. She's brought them out during fall foliage times to absolutely majestic scenery, and she's given them wedding weekends full of country-friendly activities such as apple-picking, boating, skiing, and hiking. A great location can do that for you.

On the Web

See www.charmedplaces.com to get in touch with Sarah, and tell her I sent you.

For any location you're considering, ask the same questions you did of your ceremony site (see pages 119–20), and add in the kinds of things you'll need to suit your reception's needs:

- *Is there access to electricity for the band, the chef, lighting?*
- *Are there adequate restrooms, or will we need to rent portable facilities?*
- *Is there parking?*
- *Will we need to get permits for use of a park or garden, for outdoor cooking, for liquor consumption?*
- *What's the privacy level? Especially at beach areas, will you want hordes of vacationers looking at you, or even walking up to help themselves to your buffet or bar?*
- *Is there an airport nearby? Don't laugh. Some outdoor weddings find themselves right in a flight path, with deafening noise every three minutes.*
- *Is there air-conditioning or heat, or will you have to bring in machines for that?*
- *Is the place easily accessible? Will you have to drive on fire roads to get there?*
- *Would the directions to the site be easy to follow?*
- *What about insects? Will it be mosquito season? Can citronella torches do the trick?*
- *Can you set up a tent on the grounds? Some parks, gardens, estate homes, and beaches do not allow guests to spike tents into the ground.*
- *How's the scenery? Will the leaves on the trees be turning colors?*

As with any other location, check to see that the place is kept in good condition, that any planned refurbishments will be completed by the date of your wedding, and that the staff seems to be on the ball. You can tell a lot by the friendliness and professionalism of the site manager who escorts you through the place. Do you feel welcome? Are your questions being answered? Does the manager seem willing to please you? What you want is a manager who can make your wishes come true, and who will be totally forthcoming.

Keep in mind that it's best if yours is the only wedding taking place at a location that day, at that time. When you book yourselves into a "wedding factory" you can expect scattered service, noise from the party next door, jammed parking, and a line in the parking lot when both events let out at the same time. This is not to say that all hotels that do two weddings at once are going to give you crappy service. But it's best to avoid those situations where you'll just be a number. Try to be the only party that day.

And last but not least . . . how does that site make things easier on the wedding day? If your reception will be right at the hotel where your guests are staying, then that makes life simpler for all of you. You won't have to transport them or expect them to transport themselves. Guests get a little grumbly when you ask them to drive an hour to your ceremony site, then another hour to the reception site, then two hours home again. So think about how the location can work for, rather than against, you.

Some couples marry right at their reception site. Some get a suite at the hotel where they can dress for the wedding and then return to the room right after the ceremony for alone time. After the reception, that's their honeymoon suite. In short, *no limos! No transportation at all!* How's that for avoiding bad weather and big-time car fees? Keep in mind that one hotel with a poolside terrace, a glass atrium, a piano bar, beautiful suites, and a magnificent ballroom could be an all-inclusive wedding location.

Setting It Up

Any site you choose is going to need at least some priming. I'll start you off through the process of building your site itself . . . whether you're actually creating it with a tent and walkways, lighting outside and inside areas, or just sprucing up a bare ballroom with personalized décor-related touches.

The Full Job

If you'll marry outside, whether on the beach, in a garden, or in your backyard, you'll be smart to put up some shelter. That means a tent, flooring, perhaps even walkways if the grounds have muddy paths, protruding tree roots, or a gravel walkway you don't want your guests to have to deal with.

There are loads of different types of rental tents to consider, plus all the extras like see-through ceilings, mesh walls for bug and wind protection, decorative liners to hide the pole attachments at the top. Tent designers have been in overdrive the past few years, and now you'll find tents that can be designed to fit any shape of yard, any height. And in any color you have in mind. (But please don't go for the big-top look!)

Remember that you might need more than one tent. Your caterer might need one so that his or her food prep work is hidden from view, and you might wish to get another to make that portable toilet area more attractive from the outside.

On the Web

Start your search for the best tent specialist near you at the American Rental Association Web site, www.ararental.org.

Read up on the types of structures there are to choose from, fabrics, wind and rain protection features, even the kinds of flooring you can get for the dance floor or the entire base of your site.

For walkways, you can rent them or make them out of wood with carpeting or faux golf-course-greens material. You can stake torches on the pathway or rig lighting in the trees and nearby buildings.

A true outdoor site means you're designing the *entire* thing, and lighting will be one of the most important elements. Look into hiring lighting experts to pinpoint, spotlight, floodlight, and provide glow for your entire area. Walkways and the path to the restroom need to be clearly defined, and your party area can be transformed by light alone to look extra-impressive. If you'll be by an outside swimming pool, have them flick on the underwater lights for that Club-Med-blue glow. Or line the branches of nearby trees with little white fairy lights (like Tavern on the Green in New York City). If the garden or estate home has fountains, have them turn on the lights for those as well.

I can't emphasize enough that lighting is *it* when you're creating your reception site. Party planners tell me that lighting can make a plain site more alluring and exciting. Use "gobo lights," which are specially designed discs that slip over spotlights to project images or words onto any surface. You might have your initials projected onto the side of your tent, onto the dance floor, or onto the surface of a pool. More elaborate gobo lights might project a waterfall onto a bare wall, giving you an amazing image and décor at very little expense. They can be used to project:

- Undersea scenes
- Forests
- Moroccan rug designs (to make a plain dance floor look like a priceless rug)
- Pyramids
- Monet paintings
- Oceans and beach scenes
- The wedding date
- The couple's names

Gobo designers can do it all, and they have it all at your disposal. So check with the experts to see what you can do with light, no matter where your reception will be located.

Once your site is lit, you'll also need to make it functional. That means renting tables, chairs, linens, cutlery, glasses—*everything* you'll need for the reception itself. Here's where the expenses can add up. Not only are you renting a tent, but you're renting everything in the tent. Anything anyone touches in that room is on your dime. That's what makes it different from booking a traditional ballroom or restaurant. You choose every element from the ground up. Here's what you're looking at:

- *Tables:* Choose from rounds, squares, long tables, and 8-, 10-, and 12-seaters. Tables don't have to be uniform in size and shape. Mixing it up can allow you to use your available space better and give guests room to move among tables. And don't forget tables for the deejay, the cake, the gifts, and other needs.
- *Chairs:* Go for comfort. Those cheapo metal folding chairs are for tailgate parties, not your wedding.
- *Linens:* Tablecloths, napkins, the works. Choose a color, and then choose a *coordinating* color for overlays and emphasis. Here's where your bride

and her mom are most likely to step in, since tablecloths probably aren't your thing. While you're stringing lights in the trees, they're more likely to be picking a beaded satin tablecloth for the cake table, and checking out fabrics for the seat covers. Still, each piece of cloth needs to be rented.

◆ *Cutlery:* Knives, forks, spoons, serving utensils. Add them all to the list, and go wild with the designs. Today's brides and grooms aren't going with the plain versions—it's fancy-cut all the way with great engravings and designs.

◆ *Glassware:* Again, it's design all the way with glasses. Oversized martini glasses are overshadowing plain wine glasses. Some color might be in the mix too, if you're going for water glasses with colored fluting or edges. The roster of rentable glassware is unbelievable, so help your bride flip through rental catalogs to find just the right kinds of accents, whether etchings, color, texture, or unique vodka glasses that sit in a little bowl of ice at the center of the table.

◆ *Heat and cold machines:* You might need an air conditioner or heater to keep the temperature just right in the tent. When the sun sets, it could get chilly.

◆ *Portable bar:* Don't forget the bar itself! Rent a nice-sized long bar with plenty of room for two or three bartenders to do their *Cocktail* routines and blend up those daiquiris.

◆ *High chairs* or booster seats for the little ones.

◆ *More items* (as listed at www.ararental.org): Some ideas: coffee urns, espresso machines, bubble-blowing machines, a wheeling table for the cake, and so on.

◆ *Portable restrooms:* You might need to go to a specialist for this, since you can find anything from a construction-site porta-potty to one of those high-tech trailers with roomy facilities, mahogany details, leather couches, and even television. Some couples even hire a restroom attendant to sit in the trailer and offer guests towels and breath mints. Those are the polar opposites in the world of portable toilets, so select whatever works best for your site.

Not Everything's Up to You, but Almost

Some establishments with outdoor wedding facilities do offer you the use of their own indoor party rooms. Perhaps their ballroom has big French doors that open out to the terrace or grounds. You can use their tables, chairs, and everything either indoors or out. What you'll need to rent will be more limited, but you'll still need to arrange where everything will be placed. In this case, work with the site manager to review their stock. See what the chairs are like, choose from their supply of linens to get just the right color and quality, and pick the fine wineglasses over the everyday ones.

While You Were Out

Have you seen that home-makeover show where the unsuspecting spouse leaves his or her home for the weekend and comes back to find a room or backyard completely changed by a team of designers? That's what your own house could look like when you take on the task of holding your wedding there. At-home weddings are increasing in popularity, sometimes bringing a meaningful family moment into the same setting where you grew up. Families love the at-home wedding for its sentimentality and how gorgeous the place looks once the transformation is complete. And you could get married in the same yard where you played wiffle ball, climbed trees, caught frogs, and held parties when your parents were away for the weekend. (Talk about "while you were out"!) Now, you can add another rocking good time to your homestead's memory bank when you bring your wedding to your own backyard.

Transforming a home or backyard into a wedding wonderland means another big shopping trip at the rental agency, and it also means prepping your space for the party. You might hire a professional cleaning team to spot-detail your place, landscapers to get the lawn and garden in order, and finally get that decrepit swing set out of the yard. Families who will host at-home weddings sometimes start a year in advance, taking the initiative to put in those hardwood floors, replace the carpeting in the living room, put in a rose trellis, or redo the driveway—all to get ready for your big day. When the jobs are done, when that tent is

> **What to Watch For**
>
> With throngs of guests and wedding experts traipsing through the house, it's smart practice to lock any valuables, such as jewelry and cash, away in a safe. And in the interest of safety, check with your insurance agent to see if you should get a rider for special events held in your home (see page 37 for liability policies).

up and the lighting in place, the décor set, and the sprinklers turned to *off*, your at-home wedding setting is good to go.

Have your home ready for guests: There should be hand towels and extra toilet paper in the bathrooms, dishes of breath mints and toothpicks by the sink, and paper towels in the kitchen for any spills. Set several trash containers around, such as by the bar, and appoint someone to keep a lookout for when trash bags need to be replaced. Stock your freezer with bags of ice cubes, and make sure there's plenty of room in the kitchen for the caterer to work. That might mean clearing countertops and the fridge, and freeing up electrical outlets by putting away the toaster.

Out in the Wide Open

Anytime part or all of your reception activities will take place outside, you'll need to check the terrace, stairs, and lawn for safety hazards and general appearance. Fill in those gopher holes and get rid of the dog's deposits in the backyard. Ask friends to help with the weeding, or hire a professional to take care of that. Fix a shaky handrail, check the deck for splinter potential, and clean off any yard furniture and umbrellas you might be using.

The Bare Ballroom

When the ballroom doors open up to you, you'll face a bare-bones room with nice carpeting, a lovely chandelier, plain tables and chairs, and neutral-colored walls.

This is your starting point. From here, you (or your bride) will choose table linens in theme-appropriate colors and nice fabrics, centerpieces in whatever style of floral or nonfloral design she likes (including candles, mirrors, lighted centers, and even branches and fruits, and nuts and gourds that make up the new style of centerpieces. A florist or designer can lead the way if you are uncertain about this aspect.)

You're more likely to be into the lighting of the room and the layout. Where will the band or deejay be located? How will the tables be arranged? Where do you want the food stations during the cocktail hour? Where will coffee be served? These kinds of functional decisions are more likely to be yours than "selecting the color of the centerpieces roses." It might be helpful to create a template—cut-out squares of paper to match the dimensions of the dance floor, the bar, the deejay area, the seating area—and build your reception layout from that. Or you can use a wedding-planning software program that provides the same interactive tool, where you can click and drag those tables into the arrangement that works best for you. Once you've gotten everything where you want it, save it and then share your room design with the site manager.

Seating Arrangements

With your template, you'll be able to place exactly the number and shapes of guest tables where you want them. Here comes the fun part: deciding where to seat your guests and with whom to seat them. If you haven't been warned already, you should know that this can be one of the trickiest parts of planning your reception. And you might be shocked at just how tricky it can be.

Now, you're a guy. You don't care who in the family isn't speaking to whom. You don't know that Uncle Ted hasn't spoken to Uncle Pete for twenty years because of a bad tip on a horse, and you might get knocked out of the way by your mother if you try to seat those two together at the same table. It just isn't done.

It sounds ridiculous, but creating the table seating chart is going to open up a can of worms. You'll find out about every stupid conflict among your guests. Add in divorced parents with new flames, and it can get ugly. At which "main table" do you seat your father and his new twenty-year-old girlfriend? Do you seat your mother far enough away so that she can't kill said new girlfriend with a well-aimed twenty-pound centerpiece? Do you seat Aunt Henrietta as far from the bar as possible so that she doesn't have her own private party with the Yukon Jack?

Who cares?!

This is family diplomacy at its finest. Someone in your inner circle might care a lot, and you might want to burst a blood vessel rather than sit around for yet another hour trying Aunt Henrietta at all the farthest tables from the bar. But your group knows what happened at the last wedding. It may seem so "soap-operalike" to you, but all your guests brought into one room can bring with them more backstory than you might imagine. So do yourself a favor . . . don't ask questions. Just find the solution. Your fiancée, mother, mother-in-law, and everyone else in the know about your guests' particular grudge matches and simmering resentments will let you know when you've got it right.

Aside from the pre-emptive seating plans, you'll also get the chance to do some strategic seating in a positive way. You might want your buddies to be seated with your bride's hot female co-workers. Now there's a table with sexual tension buzzing all over it. Advantageous reception seating can make your friends very happy; it's brought together plenty of happy couples before . . . even if they're just happy that night, and the next day when they have great stories to tell.

We'll get into more specifics of your reception plans in later chapters. For now, it's just important that you have your space reserved and your style of reception planned out. While the bride and her mom are most likely to get into the decorations, you do have a say in what stays and what goes. Ice sculpture of Cupid aiming an arrow? Feel free to veto that one. A cake shaped like Cinderella's castle? Since it's just going to get cut and eaten anyway, you might want to let your bride have her dream come true. So let it slide with a "Yes, dear." Work with her where you can, but trust your instincts when it comes to the fluffier side of the reception plans.

11

◇ ◇ ◇

Put It in Writing: Invitations

You might or might not be involved with your bride in choosing and designing the invitations for your wedding, but I've included this basic primer on invites in case you are doing the search with her *or* if you'll take on the task of creating your invitations as one of your "Honey, I'll do it" projects. Many of today's grooms want in on anything having to do with the computer, and making wedding invitations, place cards, and other items that can be printed out is way up there on their task list. So read on to find what you need to know about the decorative and etiquette-sensitive world of wedding invitations.

What Does the Invitation Do?

It seems like a "Duh!" question. Obviously, the invitation gives the who, what, when, and where for the wedding itself. But what you might not be aware of is that the invitation also tells the guests the style and formality of your wedding so that they know what to expect. One look at an ultraformal invitation on a cream-colored card with black swirly print, and one look at the time of the ceremony, and I know that this is going to be a formal wedding. I know you're having a dinner, not a luncheon, so I know to wear a more formal dress. Similarly, if your invitation is a playful light green one with starfish on it and more casual wording talking about toasting your wedding by the shore, I know your beach wedding will require me to wear a light sundress and bring my sunscreen. That little invitation contains a lot more information than you might expect.

What Do We Need to Know First?

You need to know a lot about your wedding before you take your first look at invitations: the formality level, the style, the theme, the date, the day of the week, and the times and exact locations of the ceremony and reception. You also need to know by when responses must be in hand and who's going to accept the RSVPs. And of course you need to know how many guests you're inviting. You can't order until you have all this figured out.

Still another thing you have to decide is who will be listed as the hosts on your invitation. If you and your bride have planned and paid for everything, you're the hosts and your names go first, as in "Sarah Smith and David Johnson request the honor of your company as they unite in marriage . . . "

If your bride's parents have bankrolled most of the wedding and have been the main planners, then they're listed first. If your parents took an equal role, or if they were the main planners, then their names go as hosts as well. Some parents might flip out if they're not listed on the invitations as hosts of your wedding. Since it can mean so much to them, nail down with your fiancée exactly who's going to be named on the invitations and how you'll write out their names. In the case of divorced parents, there's a specific way to do it. (See pages 156–59 for more on the standard models. Determine your hosts before you choose the invitation style.)

How Many Invitations Do We Need?

Whip out your guest list and start grouping names according to who gets their own invitations. Ideally, you'll order ten to fifteen extras, just to have some on hand for keepsakes (mothers and grandmothers will keep their own, of course, but there are definite craft projects involved here). These are the general rules for figuring out who on your guest list gets his or her own invitation, and who gets grouped together on one:

- Married couples receive one invitation, addressed as *Mr. and Mrs.* _____.

- Young adults over age eighteen get their own individual invitations as well. (Some couples choose to list children age sixteen and over.)
- Children under age eighteen (or sixteen) are listed by name on their parents' invitations.
- Bridal party members get their own official invitations, even though you know that they're aware of the date, time, and place. They still have to be officially invited and informed whether to bring a guest.
- The officiant usually gets an invitation, with guest optional.
- "And Guest" is included on an invitation you're sending to a friend who gets to bring a date. Or, you can find out your friend's date's name and send her or him an individual card.

The Hunt Begins

Once you're squared away with the vitals and the number of invitations you need, you can start looking around at invitation Web sites, in invitation catalogs and sample books at the stationers, and through brochures you can order out of bridal magazines. For a look at several of my favorites, go to www.invitations4sale.com and www.vismarainvitations.com. You'll also find dozens of additional Web sites to surf when you flip through the bridal magazines that are stacked up on your bride's coffee table. It's smart to check around, so that you can see the styles (and prices!) of invitations out there—from formal and classy ones to playful and informal.

Once you get a feel for the offerings, you can get deeper into the details.

It's All in the Paper

Did you know that the type of material, or card stock, your invitation comes in can affect the price by 30 percent or more? Some papers are obviously more expensive than others, and when you add in extra layers like glassy vellum coverings and speckled rice paper overlays, the prices jump.

Here's a little test: You'll see listings for 100 percent cotton paper invitations. Sounds like that would be an economical choice, right? Wrong. One of the most expensive card stocks out there is 100 percent cotton. Here's a look into the world of invitation papers, which is only the first of several price-affecting elements:

- *100 percent cotton:* The most common type of invitation paper, this is also among the priciest.
- *Corrugated:* A much thicker paper, this has a "homemade paper" look.
- *Jacquard:* A very elegant style, looks like an overlay of fabric or lace on sections or the entire invitation.
- *Laid:* A smoother blend, like all-cotton paper, but with more texture. (Please don't say "I want to get laid" too loudly in the stationers!)
- *Linen:* Boxed stationery is often made of this fine classic paper, which is also highly popular for wedding invitations. It takes print well and is lighter in weight than most other types of paper. (This also makes linen a great choice when you consider the weight of the invitations when it's time to pay the postage.)
- *Moiré:* A smooth-finish paper with watermarks pressed into it.
- *Parchment:* A heavier paper that holds print well and imparts a romantic, Old World style to your invitations.
- *Recycled Blend:* High-quality look in a variety of textures and finishes. Ask your invitation dealer for explanations of recycled paper choices and see a sample before ordering.

Know When to Fold

Another question is the shape of the invitation. Will it be one single card or a folded invitation? When you're researching the styles, check out the difference between *square fold* (a single page that folds into a square envelope, with the invitation printed inside) or *gatefold* (the outer thirds of the paper are folded inward to enclose the invitation inside; the flaps open up like a gate). Also available is the *vellum wrap*, in which an outside vellum layer is folded and attached to enclose your invitation. Other styles are out there, including scrolls, geometric shapes, scalloped edges, and ovals with shiny borders. Design possibilities are endless, so spend some time looking around.

What's Your Type?

The type and technique used for professional invitations can make a big difference in price. Here are the main procedures used to create invitations:

- *Engraved:* The most expensive and formal of options, this style features raised lettering on the front of the invitation and letter indentations on the back of the invitation. *Note:* This style is expensive and usually reserved for only the most formal of weddings.
- *Thermographed:* Thermographed invitations offer a look similar to that of engraved invitations, only there are no indentations on the back of the card. The simpler printing process means a less expensive invitation, and it may even take less time to complete your order. These elements make thermographed invitations the most popular these days.
- *Calligraphy:* Handwritten in ornate script fonts, invitations crafted this way say "I spent some bucks." Of course, you could make them a do-it-yourself job if you have great handwriting, or ask an artsy friend to write out your invitations and envelopes as a wedding gift to you. Many couples who go the calligraphy route have their artistic friends create *one* invitation, and then they take that one to a high-quality printer to have the rest printed up on great paper.

Time-Saver

Of course, you could also use your home computer to print up your choice of wording and try it out in hundreds of different fonts, font sizes, and print styles. Then, after printing out your master, you can take it to a good copy shop to have your invitations made inexpensively on top-quality paper.

Where Do We Get This Paper?

You can find and order top-quality artistic paper on the Internet, where you can select among the same imported, exotic papers used by custom invitation designers. Order a pack of beautiful Thai rice paper, or Egyptian vellum, inlaid paper, or other types, and use one of these great stocks to create your printed wedding materials.

If you'd rather shop closer to home, check out stationery stores for a wide range of colors, or go to your local office supply shop (like OfficeMax, Office Depot, or Staples) for packaged papers with theme or bridal borders, graphics, folds, and glossy shine. Stay away from the cheesier wedding papers (like the ones with the giant wedding bells) and go for elegant simplicity, pearlized colors and borders, and classy accents. You might even find coordinating envelopes that work well for less formal invitations.

Font Styles

Whether it's on your computer or in an invitation catalog, the style of font is going to determine the way your writing looks on the card. These fonts may range from traditional wedding italics to more ornate gothic lettering and a range of other swirly or playful styles. It's a matter of design, but the type also has to be legible so that your guests will need to be able to *read* the wording. If that great style of italics you found on your word processor renders your writing illegible (e.g., "Does that say 'marriage' or 'mattress'?") then it's not going to work. When you choose a font, be sure that all the characters are clear . . . especially the numbers in any times or addresses. In some fonts, 9s can look like 1s, and 1s like 9s, or 3s like 5s.

Also, keep in mind that you can mix fonts and use two. One would set your names apart from the rest of the wedding details on the invitation. For a good look at some popular font mixings, go to www.vismarainvitations.com to see the stylish pairings of Lucia and Garamond, Piranesi and Kabel, Viant and Centaur, and Yonkers and Copperplate. Other mix-and-matches can be arranged, according to your invitation company's supply or your computer's font availability.

Leslie Vismara of Vismara Invitations (see opposite page) shares with you just a sampling of how these different fonts can look on the page:

A candlelight wedding in November or an afternoon wedding on the beach each conjure up a unique style. Think of your typography in the same way. For your big event, what personality do you want to convey to your friends and family? Whether you choose an elegant script or a classic serif font, that choice will contribute to the tone of your entire celebration.

So have a little fun while you make your selection. We like to mix and match fonts for additional interest.

MIX & MATCH

Here are some of our favorite combinations

Lucia
GARAMOND

·

Piranesi
KABEL

·

Shelley
CENTAUR

·

Kuenstler
COPPERPLATE

Script Fonts

BERTHOLD	Here's to Love and laughter & happily ever after. 123456789
EMBASSY	Here's to Love and laughter & happily ever after. 123456789
KUENSTLER	Here's to Love and laughter & happily ever after. 123456789
LUCIA	Here's to Love and laughter & happily ever after. 123456789
NUPTUAL	Here's to Love and laughter & happily ever after. 123456789
PALACE	Here's to Love and laughter & happily ever after. 123456789
PIRANESI	Here's to Love and laughter & happily ever after. 123456789
SHELLEY	Here's to Love and laughter & happily ever after. 123456789
STUYVESANT	Here's to Love and laughter & happily ever after. 123456789

Serif Fonts

CENTAUR	HERE'S TO LOVE AND LAUGHTER & HAPPILY EVER AFTER. 123456789
C: ITALIC	Here's to Love and laughter & happily ever after. 123456789
COPPERPLATE	HERE'S TO LOVE AND LAUGHTER & HAPPILY EVER AFTER. 123456789
GARAMOND	HERE'S TO LOVE AND LAUGHTER & HAPPILY EVER AFTER. 123456789
G: ITALIC	Here's to Love and laughter & happily ever after. 123456789

Sans Serif Fonts

| AVENIR | HERE'S TO LOVE AND LAUGHTER & HAPPILY EVER AFTER. 123456789 |
| KABEL | HERE'S TO LOVE AND LAUGHTER & HAPPILY EVER AFTER. 123456789 |

Real Men Do Use Purple

While black is the standard invitation print color, and also one of the least expensive for its customary use, using colored inks is becoming all the rage, even in the most formal of invitations, which used to be printed *only* in black. Now you'll find a wide range of color options, such as deep purples, burgundies, navies, reds, hunter greens, and other catchy colors. If you feel like flouting the traditional rules, go with a splash of color. If tradition is your game, stick with black print on white or ecru cards.

Leslie Vismara says that today's brides and grooms are veering away from basic black and using color in greater numbers. It's a way to be more visual, and to have some fun with the design of an invitation. Plus, since invitation papers are available in richer colors, using black ink would just "clash." Better to go with the eggplant color or the romantic reds.

A Matter of Style

The style of your invitation will need to reflect the style of your wedding, and the colors may work with your chosen color scheme for the day. And then there are your personalities. Your bride may love calla lilies or roses, and she may want them as part of her invitation design. Maybe you gave her pink roses the first time you got her flowers, and she wants your wedding invitations to feature pink roses. When combing through the many style offerings, look for personalized features like that. For your beach wedding, you might want starfish, sandcastles, or a lighthouse. For your winery-based wedding, it could be a bunch of grapes or grape leaves, bottles of wine, or a picture of a winery trellis. Your choice of graphics can set the initial tone for your personalized style of wedding.

Some other style considerations that affect the price of the invitations are:

- *Go for a simpler style*: A plain invitation with a delicate border for accent looks a lot more impressive than one with a busier design, lots of embossed graphics, and too many colors.

- *Go smaller:* Oversized invitations aren't easy for guests to carry with them to the wedding, and they'll cost more to mail.
- *Skip the glitter:* It's just annoying and gets all over everything.
- *Do border patrol:* When looking at borders for your invitations, look at shaded or pearlized borders, thin black lines with a little scroll to them, or a barely-there border of daisies or roses. Your word processing program offers a range of borders to choose from, so keep this in mind if you're doing it yourself.

Insert This . . .

It's not the invitation alone that goes into the envelope. The long-lasting tradition of wedding invitations and the way-things-are-done mean that you'll be tucking into that envelope any of the following items for your guests' use or return to you:

Response Cards

The favor of a reply is requested by
Sunday, the first of May
_____ will attend
_____ will not attend

Reception Cards

Note: to be used if only *some* of your guests will be invited to both your ceremony and your reception. (Your official invitation for this split guest list, then, will include only information on the ceremony itself.)

Reception
following cocktail party
at
The Hyatt Regency
New York City
Seven o'clock in the evening

Hotel Information Cards

These cards let your guests know where they can book their hotel rooms, or the name under which you've booked a block of rooms on their behalf, hotel room prices, the reservations Web site and phone number, and the availability of non-smoking and handicapped-accessible rooms, cribs, cots, and parking information.

Printed Directions to Your Locations

Ideally, your ceremony and reception sites will already have driving directions printed out on little sheets of paper for you to distribute to your guests. If not, or if you'll be holding your wedding at home or at a nonestablishment location, you can make these yourself on your home computer *or* order professionally made maps or sheets with directions.

What to Watch For

Make sure the directions are correct! Do a drive-through in the local area to be sure that exit numbers are correct or that road construction won't send your guests detouring into the wilderness to end up lost. To avoid this eventuality, some couples include their cell-phone number on these sheets.

Grooms *love* putting together printed directions and even creating personalized maps for their guests' use. I spoke with Leslie Vismara about the flood of grooms who are coming to her company to design custom maps for the wedding-weekend destinations. Leslie says men are wild about giving directions, and also doing it in a fun graphic way using special icons to show the location of ceremony and reception sites. Check out Leslie's site to see some samples of personalized maps, and prepare to make your own. It's a service your bride (and your guests) will appreciate come the big day.

An At-Home Card

This card shares your new address and phone number for after the wedding, and perhaps the announcement of your bride's taking your name:

Kenneth and Jennifer Larson
306 Sullivan Street, Apartment 6A
Anaheim, California
(908) 555-0000

Invitation Cards

If your wedding weekend will also include other events, such as a family softball tournament, a barbecue dinner, brunch, and so on, enclose invitations or one printed itinerary to all events here. And be sure to let guests know if any dinners or brunches will be informal or formal, so they can pack the right outfits and shoes, or bring their golf clubs, tennis racquets, or other equipment.

You are invited
To a pre-wedding brunch
In the main dining room of the Westin Hotel
Saturday morning
7A.M.–9A.M.
Dress is casual.
Mr. and Mrs. Reynolds are hosting this event.

Envelopes

Most ordered invitation packages come with their own matching inner and outer envelopes. The inner envelope holds the entire invitations packet assembly, with the names of the guests invited written on the outside of it; the entire packet slides into the outer envelope. The third envelope in your packet is for the return of the response card, and you'll put a single first-class stamp on that one.

In the world of wedding envelopes, you'll find that your chosen style of invitation can come with the option of lined or unlined inner envelopes. If you have the choice, skip the lining. Some liners don't really match the invitation and are therefore an unnecessary expense. Plus, a thick lining just adds to the weight of the package and makes very little impression on your guests. Most won't even notice that your invitation envelope is lined in pink before they toss it in the trash.

As for the correct number of envelopes to order, go for plenty of extras. When you're addressing envelopes by hand (as you should do, formally), you might mess up and require a do-over. These extra envelopes should be ordered with your invitation packets, so be sure to get plenty to allow for mistakes. And yes, you can cheat and put them through your computer's printer. Just try with one first to see if the laser or the machine's heat seals the envelope while it's printing. If it does, you're back to handwriting them.

What to Watch For

Using a printer to address your envelopes in attractive fonts is acceptable now, but be smooth about it. Make sure it looks good—no smudges—and don't use labels! Sure, your mail-merge program can whip out your entire address book contents onto labels, but no self-respecting engaged couple should use labels on their invitations packet. Ever!

Keep it simple. Go with a plain outer envelope. Styles with raised décor, borders, design prints, and (shudder) glitter on the outside are not only tacky and giggle-worthy to your more classy guests, they can also cause major problems at the post office. Thick, detailed envelopes can jam up postal-processing machines or even challenge automated routing machines with lettering that cannot be recognized by scanners. Your LOVE stamps might get covered over by hand-canceling at the post office when the system can't process your packets.

That's *Doctor* Jones to You

No abbreviations are to be used on wedding invitations. See? I told you things are etiquette-driven in the invitations world.

When writing out envelopes, *all* abbreviations are spelled out, guests are addressed by their correct titles, and state names are not abbreviated. So that's *Doctor Lawrence Anson* in *Detroit, Michigan*, and the wedding is at *six o'clock in the evening*, not at six P.M.

Time-Saver

If you don't have a guest's home zip code in your address book, simply use the zip code finder at the U.S. Postal Service's Web site, www.usps.gov, to locate the correct zip-plus-four numbers.

Stamp It Out

Wedding invitations get wedding postage stamps. They could be LOVE stamps as issued by the post office, or you might go with a theme-appropriate stamp like a beach ball for your beach wedding, a flower for your garden wedding, or a Christmas stamp for your Christmastime wedding. Check at the post office or at the postal service's Web site to see which special-issue stamps are available for this important mailing.

And speaking of important, you'll need to make sure you have the right denomination of postage for your wedding-invitation packets. After you've stuffed each one with the inserts and double envelopes (hopefully, you've chosen a lightweight card stock), you'll take just one complete packet to the post office to get it weighed and measured to determine the postage needed. Record that number, and get enough stamps for all the packets, *plus enough first-class stamps for the response envelope inside the packet.* That's one of the little things frazzled brides and grooms often forget!

While you're there, ask the postal clerk whether your invitation packet is going to be a challenge to the scanning machines. If you've bound your invitation packs with a tie or clasp inside, that raised metal piece could be a problem. So get the okay before you cause a postal dilemma.

The Writing of the Invitation

Okay, now that you know what to include with your invitations, what kind of design and ink you'll be using, and, how to figure out the postage, it's time to get into the wonderful world of invitation etiquette once more. And this time it's serious. The rules for wording invitations are rock solid. You *must* adhere to these according to your wedding's formality, since this is one of the few areas where traditional rules still apply.

Back to Who's Hosting

I touched on it before, but here are some details. When you're dealing with formal invitations, you must use full formal titles for everyone named and spell out all abbreviations. Look through the examples in order to properly credit the parents who are to be listed on your invitations:

If the bride's parents are hosting the wedding:

Mr. and Mrs. Samuel Davids
request the honour of your presence
at the marriage of their daughter
Erin Marie
and
Nicholas Michael Gathers
son of
Mr. and Mrs. Michael Gathers
Saturday, the twentieth of June
at four o'clock in the afternoon

Saint Cecile's Church
15 Main Street
Philadelphia, Pennsylvania

If both sets of parents are sharing hosting responsibilities equally:

Mr. and Mrs. Erik Gregory
and
Mr. and Mrs. Benjamin Gomez
request the honour of your company
at the marriage of their children
Therese Juliette
and
Warren Richard
[etc.]

When divorced parents of the bride are hosting:

Mr. Paul Stevens
and
Mrs. Renee Stevens
request the honour of your company
at the wedding of their daughter
Renata Elise
to
Mr. James Kevin Warrington
[etc.]

When multiple sets of the bride's parents are hosting, such as the very common situation of divorced and remarried parents, a group title is often used in place of the lengthier list of four or more names:

The loving parents of
Wendy Anne Nichols
request the honour of your company
as their daughter unites in marriage with
Mr. Vincent Alan Montgomery
[etc.]

When the couple is planning, paying for, and hosting their own wedding:

Ms. Susan Marie Vickers
and
Mr. Quincy Aaron Harrold
Request the honour of your presence
as they unite in marriage
[etc.]

When the couple is planning, paying for, and hosting their own wedding—but they still want to honor their parents on the invitation, they might write it like this:

Ms. Lisa Anne Jeffries
and
Mr. Paul Michael Johnson
together with their families,
Request the honour of your presence
as they unite in marriage
[etc.]

These samples, of course, are just models of "the way it's done" with formal invitations. If your wedding will be less formal, you can word the invitation however you'd like, provided it contains all the necessary information. So your wedding on a yacht might feature an invitation like this one:

Come sail with us into the sunset
As we join together in marriage
On the yacht
Richard Robinson
In Newport, Rhode Island
On Saturday, the third of August
At 6:00 P.M.
[etc.]

What to Watch For

Don't try to cram too many lines into your invitation. Going with smaller type and including too much detail will only make your invitations strange-looking and hard to read. Ask the invitations expert you're dealing with to do yours up in "photo lettering," which is a process that sizes your invitation lines to the page, spreads everything out evenly, and makes the invitation look more centered and organized.

RSVPs

When your guests reply with their yes or no responses is when you'll tally your final head count. You'll give this magic number to your caterer, baker, and other wedding professionals so that they can charge you an arm and a leg for each one.

Get that number way in advance by setting an early RSVP date, and then follow up with invited guests who haven't gotten back to you by then. Before you ask, e-mailed RSVP options are increasingly popular, but some couples still prefer having those little response cards in hand. You never know when someone's e-mail hasn't come through; and you can bet that few of your elderly relatives have e-mail accounts. If you know your guests will have no problem responding, you can set up an RSVP account through an online invitation tracker.

Save-the-Date Cards

If your wedding will be held during a particularly busy time of the year, or if you know your friends and family are jet-setters with packed schedules, it's probably a good idea for you and your bride to send out save-the-date cards. These formal

or informal announcements ask everyone on your list to keep your wedding date open on *their* schedules.

Save-the-date cards can be formal, ordered in the style of your invitation packet as part of the entire package, or you can design an entirely different style of card at this point in the planning stage. One great idea to really put your own stamp on this announcement is to create a save-the-date brochure. I spoke with Janet Holian, vice president of marketing for VistaPrint.com (www.vistaprint. com), about this hot new trend and why more of today's couples are going for the glossy foldouts to get the job done. While traditional save-the-date cards or postcards were basic and to the point, the new brochures give an added kick to your announcement. Janet says, "With a brochure, you can include a color photo of the two of you on the cover, the basic information on when and where both the ceremony and reception will be held, suggested attire, *and* a page on that great story about how you proposed." The sample brochure Janet sent me showed the engaged couple smiling from the front cover, the vitals of their upcoming event, the engagement story, two detailed maps of the area with the hotel and other important locales starred, some history about the area where the wedding would take place, information on the hotel room block, contact information for the hotel, contact information for the bride and groom, and the Web site for the couple's own personalized wedding page. This one attractive brochure gave future guests everything they needed to know, plus some fun FYIs to get them excited about the couple's wedding weekend before the official invitations arrive later.

Placing Your Order

You're all set to go! If you're ordering your invitations rather than making them yourself, you'll need to make sure your order form is complete, triple-checked for accurate spelling (don't get your mother-in-law's name wrong!), ordered in ample time, and paid for with a credit card. Be sure to check the finished invitations for errors and allow enough time for reprinting if necessary. Any mistakes the printing company makes is on their dime to correct, not yours. That's why it's important to hang on to your printed order form. And be sure there's still enough time to address and stuff the envelopes.

Ordering Online

A quick note on ordering your invitations if you decide to use an online supplier: Be sure the site is secure, established with an actual telephone number and street address, and that it offers a complete and solid return and refund policy. If any of these things are unavailable, find another company. Again, ask married friends for referrals, and stick with reputable industry names.

What to Watch For

You can call in your order to some invitation companies out there, but skip that! When you order, put it in print and keep a copy. That way, you can prove that you ordered invitations with the correct wedding date, and not what the sales associate *heard* you say.

When Should We Send the Invitations?

Traditionally, wedding invitations go out six to eight weeks before the wedding, but you should allow more time if your wedding will be held during the busy summer months or on a holiday weekend. If you're having a destination wedding and expect your guests to travel to your spot, give them several months of notice. The more advance notice, the greater the chance your most-wanted guests will be able to make it, and the more they'll appreciate you for respecting their schedules.

What Else Do You Need to Print Up?

Your invitations are not the only things you might have printed up for your wedding day. You already read about what goes into a wedding program, and you're now something of an expert on invitations, at-home cards, and envelopes. But there are other fun printed things that can add a bit of style to the information you need to convey. So here's a list of other items to order or make yourself on the computer using paper or card stock from office supply or craft stores:

- Thank-you notes
- Seating cards (lists guests by name and the number or name of the table they're at)
- Table-number cards (could be a number, or could be a theme word such as *Rings*, *Eternity*, or *Forever*—a trick to keep petty family members from squabbling over who gets to sit at table number 2, rather than table number 3)
- Pew cards (listing which of your most honored guests are to be seated in reserved rows)
- Menu cards (stylish cards placed on guest tables to list the courses coming up next)
- Coasters (see examples from Vismara Invitations below)

- Invitations to the rehearsal and rehearsal dinner
- Invitations to pre-wedding events
- Invitations to post-wedding events (such as coffee back at your parents' place or a continuation of the party at a nearby lounge after the official reception shuts down)
- Invitations to the bridal brunch on the morning of the wedding
- Printed cards to accompany gifts for your bridal party and parents
- Printed cards to accompany favors for guests
- Printed cards to accompany guest hotel room gift baskets
- Directional signs for the following
  - Parking areas
  - Path to the ceremony
  - Path to the reception
  - Restrooms
  - Coat check
  - Cocktail-hour room
  - Stops along the way at a traveling reception
- Additional printed signs
- Wedding programs

Time-Saver

For all of the less formal mailings you might be sending out, like invitations to the wedding brunch, the rehearsal dinner, wedding weekend activities, and so on, you might want to get a small batch of personalized return address labels printed up. They can have a bridal theme, the theme of your wedding, or you can go to www.vistaprint.com to check out their personalized caricature return labels for a fun and artsy kick to your envelopes.

If you're assuming the role of print master, then you have a lot of jobs ahead. Make it easier by learning how to mail merge or how to use Outlook to organize and print out lists and labels, maps, and calendars. What might take minutes for you to complete earns you big points on the groom-involvement scale, and we all know you're actually excited about creating those place cards in the font you choose. So get printing, buddy.

12

◇ ◇ ◇

Step On It: Transportation for the Wedding Day

YOU REALLY KNOW how to make an entrance . . . and so does your bride. On the wedding day, how you arrive is just as important as arriving on time. Needless to say, choosing the mode of transportation, picking out individual cars, and arranging pickup schedules for everyone who needs a lift is usually one of the first jobs a groom volunteers for. (Did you flip to this chapter first, by any chance?)

Here's how you'll arrange your wheels for the day. You could go traditional with a black stretch limousine, elegant with a gleaming white Rolls-Royce, or exotic with an Aston Martin or Maserati. You could go testosterone-filled with a stretch Hummer, or you could ride off with your bride hanging on to the back of your Harley. She might be dreaming of a horse-drawn glass-enclosed carriage, or you both might want to hop on board a trolley together with your bridal party for an attention-getting ride to the reception. These days, anything goes when it comes to wedding-day transportation, and more couples are choosing to go with something a little bit more exciting than a limo. So take a look at the many car-rental options out there and see if you can arrange a unique and exciting ride on the big day.

Anything but a Limousine

We'll get into the whole limousine thing in a minute, so be patient if you're a traditionalist and want to stick with the tried-and-true wedding transport. But first, I want to open up the doors to what could be a tempting collection of exotic car options. Hey, you're in charge of choosing, so why not dream big?

Exotic Cars

- Rolls-Royce
- Bentley Arnage
- Excalibur
- Lamborghini
- Mercedes Benz E420
- Aston Martin DB6 or DB7
- Jaguar E Type
- Jaguar XK8 Convertible
- BMW Z3
- Ferrari 328 GTS or 355GTS
- Ferrari F355 Spider
- Ferrari 360 Modena
- Lotus Esprit or Elise
- Morgan +8
- Porsche 911 Carrera
- Porsche 996
- Porsche Boxter
- Porsche Speedster
- TVR Griffith
- Maserati Spyder Cambiocorsa
- Viper Roadster
- Prowler Roadster
- Classic Convertible
- Thunderbird Convertible
- Classic Beetle
- Mustang Mach 1
- Shelby GT Cobra
- Audi TT Convertible
- Saab Convertible
- Boss Mustang (if you want to go retro)
- Lexus Coupe

Stretches

- Lexus GX 400 ten-passenger
- BMW 750IL ten-passenger
- Red Corvette ten-passenger
- Stretch Lincoln Navigator
- Stretch Humvee
- Stretch Beetle
- Stretch Excalibur
- Stretch Excursion
- Stretch Expedition
- Stretch Escalade
- Stretch Mercedes

Carrying a Crowd

- Thirty-passenger party bus (comes with television, surround sound, mood lighting, table, seating, and restroom for a party on wheels)

- Mini-bus
- Trolley
- SUVs: Suburban, Tahoe, Excursion, Yukon, Navigator

Her Fantasy

- Horse-drawn carriage (check with Carriage Association of America at www.caaonline.com or Carriage Operators of North America at www.cona.org to find reputable carriage rental companies and additional state associations in your area, plus a list of rules and regulations for use on city streets, in a variety of weather conditions, and so on)
- Gondola
- Private yacht
- Light-strung schooner
- Hot Air Balloon
- Horseback

Your bride has transportation fantasies too, so check with her before you book your final selection. When else will you get to ride in a Bond car? Is she really serious about riding off on horseback? Will you be embarrassed riding through your hometown in a flower-strewn horse-drawn carriage with a top-hatted driver waving to the crowd of onlookers?

Consider your options, and surf some car-rental and classic-car sites to see what's out there. And don't forget that you can rent an exotic car *for the day* and not just for the hours of the wedding. Imagine showing up at the golf course for a round with your buddies on the morning of the wedding . . . driving that Ferrari.

Now let's get back to the limousine thing. . . .

The Classic Wedding Limousine

Nothing announces "wedding" quite like a stretch limo. Its presence is a given in most wedding scenarios, and a classic part of any married couple's big-day photo albums. If you and your bride want to go limo, here are the basics.

You can find limos in several stages of stretch: eight-, ten-, and twelve-passenger cars. There are limos with mini bars, mood lighting, TVs, champagne flute holders, sun-roof options—the works. Color choices range from white to black, gray, and a new array of colors from deep plum to hot pink. Car detailers are churning out fun remodeled limos in deco colors and designs that might appeal to you.

Most limousine companies offer wedding packages that include car rentals of three, five, or seven hours, plus some freebies like a gratis champagne toast with a champagne stand and your driver popping the cork, a red carpet rolled out for your entrance after the ceremony ends, even the use of the car's musical horn playing "Here Comes the Bride" or any other number of tunes. You can request the car to be stocked with water, soft drinks, champagne, snacks, and ice if you have a long haul to the reception site, and you can even give the driver several CDs to load into the sound system. This is your big ride for your big day, so research how you can customize it. And you do know that the privacy wall in the limo isn't always soundproof, right?

Finding Your Limousine- or Car-Rental Company

Spend time researching limousine-rental companies, comparing price packages and getting a firsthand look at what you're ordering. The ages of limousines vary tremendously, and you'll want to be sure you're getting a newer model that's in great working condition and is religiously washed and waxed. The ol' bait-and-switch is alive and well in the world of limousines, so don't get tricked into finding yourself with the oldest car on the lot on your wedding day.

Asking for referrals is your best first move. Talk to recently married friends to see who they hired for their wedding days, and go beyond asking about prices. Ask if the drivers were courteous even if the couple was late, the limousines showed up on time, and the cars were in great condition. Then ask about the cost. Other people to ask for referrals:

♦ Corporate honchos who do a lot of client entertaining.
♦ Concierges at 4- or 5-star hotels who regularly book limos for their most

important guests. The next time you're in a Westin, ask the concierge who they hire to drive their clients.

* Wedding coordinators and wedding experts who have been in the business and can recommend the best names in the industry.

On the Web

Any company names that you receive through referrals or read about in the Sunday wedding section of your local paper should be checked for professional association membership. For the thumbs up and a green light to further research these companies, go to the National Limousine Association (856-596-3344, www.limo.org) or your local livery association. Limousine rental agencies who are members have a long-standing presence in the business, boast a good reputation with repeat customers, and are exposed to the latest information, training, conferences, and access to the newest features in car rentals.

Of course, it couldn't hurt to check company records with the Better Business Bureau. Any background checking you can do to ensure that your chosen companies are legitimate is a good use of your time. "Gypsy companies" do exist out there, and they often consist of two battered limos and a shady fellow who could afford an ad in the Yellow Pages. Don't fall for a scam. Make sure your limo company is the real deal.

What you're first assessing with limousine-rental companies is: the quality and condition of their cars. You're going to the lot, buddy, and get ready to look under the hoods, in the back passenger areas to be sure everything is clean and fresh-smelling. No dirty floor mats or dried-out seating for you.

Next; you're looking at price packages; be ready to see some price differentials. As I'm sure you know, going with the cheapest company isn't the smartest move. So go for the medium range in fees. Assess their packages. See how many hours they give you for how much, and—most important—find out what their overtime rates are. As many married couples can tell you, overtime is pretty much guaranteed on a day as packed as your wedding day.

Your next questions have to do with the kind of service you can expect on the wedding day. Your driver is going to be a key player. If he doesn't get you there on time, you're in hot water. You want a responsible, punctual driver who's driving a reliable car. So try to talk to the driver(s) the company is planning to assign to your wedding.

Questions to Ask the Reservations Agent

- Do you have limousines available to rent on our wedding date?
- What kind of cars do you have?
- Do you have eight-, ten-, or twelve-person, etc.?
- What are your prices for each different type?
- Do you have the model we desire? (e.g., Bentley, Rolls-Royce, and so on)
- How old are these cars?
- What colors are available?
- What are the price packages for the white versus the black ones? (At most companies, black can be less expensive than white, and gray less expensive than black. It's all about supply and demand.)
- What are the features of your standard limousine?
- Do you offer free extras, such as a champagne stand, red carpet, or balloons?
- Can we negotiate a discount if we don't want them?
- What is your overtime fee?
- Are overtime charges figured by the

- hour or by the half-hour? (Very important! Ask for the half-hour time increments so you're not paying for an hour when you were only ten minutes late!)
- Do you charge by the hour or a set fee for a length of time?
- Do you offer a refund or cancellation guarantee?
- Do you offer a budget wedding package? What is included?
- What are your rates for a party van or bus for our guests?
- Can we get a discount if we're renting a certain number of cars, plus vans or buses for our guests?
- Do you have insurance? (Ask to see an actual copy of the insurance certificate to be sure. This is no time to be lazy.)
- Do you have a liquor license, so that we can drink in the car? (Important! Some companies don't allow drinking in their cars! Plus, some states have laws about which types of cars are allowed to hold drinking passengers.)

Questions About Your Drivers

- Can we get your most experienced drivers?
- What kind of experience and training do your drivers receive? (Note: drivers need to take special training to get behind the wheel of stretch vehicles and party buses, so be sure they're licensed to drive your chosen vehicle.)
- What will the drivers be wearing? (For a formal wedding, ask that the drivers wear a tuxedo or appropriate dark suit. And let the company know if your wedding is less formal, so that your driver can wear, say, a black turtleneck and black pants.)
- Do your drivers carry two-way radios? (*Very important!* Cell phones are fine, but they can blink out in some low-reception areas. A two–way radio will connect the driver with his home base, so that contact is always assured in case of emergencies.)
- Can we get the driver's cell-phone number in case we need to get in touch with him directly? (Don't sweat this one too much, since you can always contact your driver through the company's dispatch number.)
- Do you wash and wax the car before you send it out? (Don't laugh—some companies working in a bad weather week don't take the time to stop by the car wash. You won't want a pollen-dusted car to show up for your wedding, so put this request in your order and contract to ensure a shining car!)

What to Check in the Cars Themselves

- Is this a new car?
- Is it just a few years old and still looks like new, or is it obviously aging?
- Is it well-maintained inside and out?
- Is it waxed?
- Are dents and scratches visible, or is the car nicely detailed?
- Are the ashtrays clean?
- Is the rug vacuumed?
- Is everything working? The lights? The windows? The privacy shield? The radio?
- Does it smell of cigarette smoke from recent passengers?
- Can we get a designated nonsmoking car?

This firsthand inspection of the cars is a great way to tell the quality of the company you're dealing with. The best companies treat their cars like treasures and keep them in top condition *all* the time. Pride in appearance and care for the cars is a sign that you'll get a great-looking vehicle that runs like a dream on your wedding day.

What to Watch For

If the manager won't let you look inside the cars, or if he's trying to get you to look at pictures rather than go onto the lot, run away. A good manager with nothing to hide will encourage you to look inside the company's cars until you find the one(s) you want.

Sealing the Deal

When you've given the nod, be sure to arrange for a highly detailed order form. Specify the exact cars you've chosen by make and model number, and also by the license plate number. This way, the company is obliged to give you those top-notch cars you looked at in the parking lot, and not their lemons from the back alley.

Have the sales manager write down the specifics of the package you've chosen, including times and locations of pickups, how many cars you'll need, which colors, how long you'll have them for, and so on. Overtime agreements, freebies, cancellation policies, requests for specific drivers by name—everything needs to be in print and kept in your records. Pay by credit card, keep a copy of the contract, get the rental agent's name and number, and remember to call and confirm your car reservations at least a week before the wedding.

Instructions for the Driver

If you'll be hiring several cars, you should give the limousine company a detailed and organized itinerary specifying whom they're picking up, and when and where (exact street addresses, apartment numbers, and hotel names, plus phone numbers at those locations in case the driver needs better directions). Use the worksheet in the appendix section to start your own itemized directions, and give a copy to the company and keep a duplicate. Coordinating rides on the wedding day is one of those detail-oriented tasks that needs to be iron-clad for smooth sailing.

Sample List of Limousine Logistics

- Limo #1: picks up bride and bride's father at bride's house and takes them to ceremony site
- Limo #2: picks up bridesmaids and mothers and takes them to ceremony site
- Limo #3: picks up groom, best man, ushers, and groom's family and takes them to ceremony site

- Limos #1 and #2: wait through the ceremony and then transport everyone to the reception; Limo #3 is released at this time
- Limos #1 and #2: return to reception site for return ride home

---

If you're on a budget, you can get through the day with only one limousine. It would take the bride and her father to the ceremony site while everyone else gets his or her own ride around town. The bride and groom then take that limousine to the reception site. This is a way to make your entrances without scorching your budget. These cars might come at a price of $80–$120 an hour—even more if you're going with a stretch limousine or stretch classic car. So look at your schedule to see just how *short* an amount of time you'll need these cars for, and work out alternate rides for everyone else.

There are other ways to cut your limousine costs:

- Book your cars early! Last-minute orders can cost you big money in rush fees, and you might not get the best selection of top-quality cars too close to the wedding date.

- Go for a regular limousine instead of a stretch. There are only two of you, so why book a car that holds twelve?
- Have the limousine only take the two of you from the ceremony to the reception for the best image without the biggest price tag. If you all can get to the ceremony site on your own—perhaps your bride will get ready in a side room at the site and won't need the expensive car rental to get there—then you'll save hundreds of dollars without that extra one or two hours of service . . . per car!
- Skip the earlier rides! If your ceremony and reception will be held in the same location, you might just need a quick ride home in a limo . . . or none at all if you're staying in the same hotel where the reception is taking place.
- Assess the number of cars you'll need. The bride and her father don't *have* to ride alone in the limo. The bridesmaids and flower girl can go with them. If you can cut one extra car out of your order, that's thousands of dollars saved.
- Hire a town car to pick you up after the reception, rather than a limousine. The difference might be $30–$60 per hour.
- Hire a local rental company. Since the "time is money" meter starts running from the time the car first pulls out of the company lot until the time it is checked back in, not when it picks you up and drops you off, you'll pay for any extra travel time required.
- Check out classic-car clubs in your area. They might have a member who makes a little extra cash on the side by renting out his 1920s mint-condition antique car for a small chunk of change.
- Use your own, or a friend's, cleaned-up and waxed convertibles or vans for wedding-day transport. You can decorate these cars as well, which you might not be able to do with a rented car or limo.
- Don't tip extra. Remember that most companies already include a 15–18 percent gratuity in your bill. So be aware of the fine print and don't tip twice.

Getting Rides for Others

Arranging rides for other family members (like aunts, uncles, grandparents) and for out-of-town guests could be as simple as taking helpful friends up on their offer to share their car rides with others, or reserving the use of the hotel's free shuttle. Many hotels where you've booked a block of rooms, or where you'll hold your reception or rehearsal dinner, will offer their regular guest shuttle buses to use for the ceremony, reception, and getting-back-to-the-hotel transport. Just ask whether this service is free or if they'll cut you a deal on the reservations fee.

Another option might be to hire a party bus or van from a rental company to do the same job. Recent wedding guests tell me that the party bus was the place to be after the reception ended! With its sound system, mood lighting, and festive feelings among the slightly sloshed wedding guests, the bus kept the celebration going during the long ride home.

And of course, it goes without saying that you need to provide *safe* rides home for your guests after the wedding. That shuttle bus would be perfect, but if that's not in your plans, then you can arrange to have cabs on hand after the party or give the site manager that cab company number so he can secure after-party rides for your guests.

As for you and your bride, you'll need a safe ride home at the end of the night as well. If you won't have a limo deliver you to the honeymoon suite, you or the best man can drop off your car (along with your suitcases) at the reception site earlier in the day. If you're going to be drunk, a designated driver can be your new chauffeur for the evening.

Valet Service

Don't forget to look into valet service if your reception site doesn't have a parking system of its own. If you're having an outdoor or at-home wedding, you'll do well to hire an independent valet company to work the driveway for your guests. Be aware that you might have to pay for valet service at an established hotel or banquet room, in which case you may be presented with a per-car tally at the end of the night. So ask about this ahead of time . . . and be sure to arrange with the site for its drivers *not* to accept tips from your guests. You'll cover the tips afterward.

How many valets do you need? Go for one parking attendant for every seven or eight cars. Fewer than that and your guests could be waiting in a long line at the end of the night while those few valets wheeze and fall over from too much running around. More is better. And please don't go with amateurs. Sure, your little brother's friends can do the job for $50, but professional valets are well-trained for parking and for driving different types of cars. Go pro.

When you hire a valet company, get a solid contract designating all the specifics, including times and terms of service, what the drivers will be wearing, and so on. Pay with a credit card (not a debit card) and keep your order form safe. Call to confirm a week in advance, especially if your wedding is in peak season. Also, ask to see the company's liability insurance policies to ensure that their drivers are covered for any damage to your guests' cars or to the site's property.

Decorating Cars

Decorating the bride and groom's getaway car for their post-wedding escape is a tradition that dates back to a time when weddings were an "exchange of goods." That means the bride was "sold" or "traded" to the groom as an asset. We've gotten away from that sort of medieval mindset, but we still practice some of the same symbolic rituals. Did you know that tying a string of shoes to the back bumper of the bride and groom's car goes back to when shoes were a symbol of a completed transaction? It's amazing anyone still does that anymore. Tin cans made more noise than dragging sneakers, so pretty soon it was soda cans on a string. Once someone discovered these caused sparks when they were dragged on the pavement, that went out the window too.

Today, you (or your buddies) might decorate the car with a sign that says JUST MARRIED, or have colored streamers take the place of those former dragged objects. You can write on car windows with soap or shaving cream, or visit a party-supply store for safe and temporary car window paints (like those high-schoolers use at graduation time). Don't tape anything to the car, obviously, and know that metal hinges on anything attached to the car could scrape the paint job.

13

◇ ◇ ◇

Get the Picture: Photography and Videography

PICTURES AND VIDEO of your wedding day are priceless. So that's why you're going to pay big bucks to hire professionals to snap and roll footage of your every move. There's no way around it. This is no time to ask friends to grab their digital cameras and be in the right place at the right time. Sure, you *could* do that if you're on a really rock-bottom budget, or if you're jetting off to Vegas on a whim, but you'd be risking something much bigger than you might be aware of.

You'll keep those pictures and videotaped footage of your wedding day forever. And they get more valuable over time. Just ask the long-married couple what they'd save first if their house was burning down, and you're going to hear "our photo albums." Portraits and video from that once-in-a-lifetime day are worth twenty times those exorbitant prices you're going to be quoted, so don't flip out when you read quoted packages in the thousands of dollars. When you consider how perfectly these photography and videography experts capture you, your bride, and those amazing moments you'll share, you'll be fine with the price.

On the Web

To locate accredited photographers and videographers to interview, start with the main industry associations for member names and contact information. They are:

- Professional Videographer Association of America: www.pva.to, 209-653-8307
- Professional Photographers of America: www.ppa.com, 800-786-6277
- Wedding and Portrait Photographers International: www.eventphotographers.com

Finding Photographers and Videographers

These masters of the lens should be selected through referrals, not by throwing darts at the Yellow Pages. True professionals are in high demand, and your recently married friends and family will be able to tell you which experts got the job done and which ones *still* haven't delivered the wedding video. Word-of-mouth referrals are the way to go, 100 percent. If you're the first in your clan to marry, you can rely on referrals from a wedding coordinator, from co-workers, neighbors, or anyone else whose opinion you trust.

If you go blindly to an untested expert, be sure to visit their studio, ask how long they've been in business, and look at their sample albums or videotapes to see how they've produced their work. Then—and this is important—see how you get along with the photographer and videographer. You should have good rapport. The guy (or gal) has to have the right personality and degree of professionalism *since he or she will be out there among your guests all night*. So you should hire an expert who's not only good at the craft, but will also blend in like one of your guests. You don't want a brooding *artiste* or a hyped-up control freak shouting orders all day. See if you get a good feeling from any pro you talk to. See if that pro listens to you, answers your questions, and is willing to show you his stuff, and be sure that the work is good.

Then check out the studio. Is it organized? Are piles of undelivered picture packets leaning in a tower over in the corner? Are people having heated work-related discussions on the phone? You can tell a lot about a pro from his or her space. Cluttered doesn't mean anything, since many brilliant minds work well in scattered fashion (that may be why they went into the arts) but obvious signs of chaos are bad.

What's Your Style?

The work of wedding photographers and videographers is available in a few different categories:

- *Portrait-style:* These are the pictures with everyone lined up, posing for the camera. You'll get those shots of you and your men in a lineup, and you and the bride posed in position holding your smiles. Some experts like to control the action, and their pictures (beautiful as they are) are more posed than captured.
- *Candid-style:* These picture experts know how to snap that perfect, unposed moment . . . like the second you first see your bride step into view. Magically they're there when your buddy gives you a tap on the shoulder to say "Good luck" or when your dad is coming toward you to shake your hand. Candid-style photo experts know just how to get the great shots without posing them.
- *Photojournalist-style:* Experts who shoot this way call themselves journalists for a reason. Their pictures tell a story, the narrative of your day. They grab on to a theme and run with it, letting their cameras capture your entire unspoken story.

No one style is inherently better than the other. You need to decide which style suits you best and seek potential wedding-day photographers and videographers who work in that style. You'll need to be aware of the differences and look for them in the samples these experts show you. Talk to the photo pros and ask them to explain their philosophies . . . it may sound artsy, but it's something you need to know to get the kinds of pictures you want. Some couples don't want *any* posed pictures. They want to go about their day and trust that the photographer is getting the good shots. If this is your style, appraise how the pro's style matches your idea. Get a good feel for the different kinds of shots by perusing sample photos on the Internet—you can find them on professional photographers' Web sites and couples' personalized wedding Web sites. Print out the ones you really like, and bring them to your photographer for a real-life look at your preferences.

What's Your Equipment Like?

Here's where it might get more fun for you. You're dealing with technology. Digital cameras. Image chips. Spy-size hidden microphones to attach to your lapel. Editing systems that rival those at the major television networks. Photography and videography is high tech, and you might enjoy looking into the inner workings of this world. Grooms tell me that they immediately volunteered to do photography and videography research, since it was more tech, more them, and a hell of a lot more enjoyable than picking out napkin colors. I've seen grooms mesmerized at bridal shows as they stand in front of a videographer's computer screen to watch DVDs of edited wedding footage.

So be sure to ask about the expert's cutting-edge equipment, their digital work, and their editing systems. Ask them to explain the new technology, including any *drawbacks*. For instance, the jury is still out on whether wedding footage put directly onto DVDs will fade over time, as opposed to the more lasting VHS form.

Ask about editing. Can the photographer do some touching up of your pictures to get rid of red eye (usually they can) or take that wrinkle out of her forehead when she smiles? What kind of editing will the videographer do? As a warning, you should know that some video experts go nuts with the editing and special effects. It's a way for them to play with their machines, and to charge you almost double. You don't need strobe-light effects. You don't need animated bunnies hopping across your reception footage. You don't need rave-lighting effects that weren't happening in your ballroom. And you don't need an animated dancing bunny, joining the end of the conga line. I have no idea why some videographers do these things . . . maybe it's the long hours and lack of coffee. Be sure to specify which effects you *do* want, or take the safe road and ask for no special effects at all.

What's in Your Package?

Photography and videography packages for weddings usually run in the five- to seven-hour time slots, with a certain number of portraits and albums included in your purchased plan. Look at the pro's printed wedding-day plans, and see if you can negotiate. For instance, you might be able to wangle a three-hour plan out of your picture expert for a few hundred off the top. Or, you might opt out of the parents' albums and choose instead to make them from candids or proofs.

You can negotiate to get those hundreds of proofs for free (the photographer doesn't need them after your pictures come in), and you *should* negotiate to buy or get the negatives for your pictures *as well as the master or "raw" videotape* your videographer shoots. Why do you want the masters? That's where the money is in the world of photography and videography. If you want to order 8x10s of a wedding portrait, it may cost you a few hundred dollars. Hey, the photographer owns the negatives and copyright to all of your wedding pictures (you signed the contract!) and he or she knows their value to you. So up goes the price.

What to Watch For

If you can't buy your negatives right now, ask how long the photographer will keep them on file. Some pros discard their old stock after two or three years. Have this date in mind so you can go back later to buy your negatives.

As for getting the raw, unedited video footage of your wedding in addition to or instead of your edited tape, you can use that later to have a professional edit done, or improve upon the edited version your videographer put together. Some couples have more money down the road, and they love to re-edit their wedding videotape to include footage from their honeymoons, their first anniversaries, the births of their kids, and so on. If you've purchased your raw videotape, you will have lots more to work with.

As far as the rest of your price packages, always get the most you can for your budget. Choose your own album with more pictures than the parents' albums will have. These official albums are big and glossy, exorbitantly expensive, and limited in the number of shots you can include. Most brides and grooms create additional albums with candid shots and proofs anyway, so these high-priced albums don't need to be perfect. They're a keepsake. An important keepsake and probably a new part of your coffee table décor for the first year of your marriage, but a keepsake nonetheless. Trust me . . . you're going to wind up with hundreds of proofs and candids. There will be plenty of pictures and probably several albums made out of this deal.

The Shots You Want

You and your bride might want to request specific pictures of the two of you with your families. Maybe you want a great shot with all of your high school buddies who have flown in from all over the country. You haven't seen each other in seven years, and you might not see each other again for another ten. Or your bride might have a favorite great-uncle she has adored since she was a little girl. The photographer needs to be told to get that shot. Remember, the experts don't know anyone else in the room but you, so it's wise to give them a heads up through a printed wish list of shots to get. Add this to do your to-do list: Sit down with your bride and write out the pictures and footage you want the most.

Keep in mind the possibility of getting some of your wedding pictures developed in black and white. Photos taken in color can be developed in this classic, timeless style, and many couples love to have these extremely flattering pictures in their portfolio for a day in the future when they might change their décor and bring out the black-and-white photos for display. Sepia-tone photos are also increasingly popular, as are black-and-white or sepia-tone pictures with just *some* added coloring in the frame. These are stylish, very cool, and a nice twist on traditional color pictures.

You might get fancy borders, fade-out borders that seem to blend out into a cloudy frame, or you might have your photographer use a wide-angle lens to capture a panoramic view of your wedding setting. This one is great for garden parties or locales with beautiful surrounding views and sunsets in the distance. You might ask the photographer to go up to a balcony overlooking your reception for a bird's-eye view.

Also possible are action shots, like motion-play pictures of your limo speeding off with the shutter timing planned just right in order to get the effect of streaking taillights behind your car. Photographers can work magic with lighting, lens work, and special photo tricks to make your shots unique. One growing trend is infrared selections within your larger collection of shots. These pictures capture lighting in a unique way and make your wedding scene look like something out of a movie. Another catchy technique employs a "fish-eye" lens, which expands and rounds your picture. This one's great for giving a new dimension to your ceremony and reception sites, the view of the ocean in front of your beach wedding, or a gathering of all your guests on the church steps. Ask about it. It can result in fun pictures.

Soundtracks

A well-edited wedding video will be set against great music, songs that work with your theme, reflect who you are as a couple, or hold that timeless wedding feel. Provide your videographer with a list or CDs of your favorite songs, so that he can work them into the finished product.

It's in the Timing

Smart wedding couples tell me that they make better use of time on their wedding day by having some of the professional pictures taken *before* the ceremony, so that they don't miss their entire cocktail hour posing for all those mandatory shots. Have your photographer go to your bride's location to take all the pre-pix with her and her family, then come to where you and the guys are for your pictures. The rest can be done later. You'll save time and get more out of your day.

Another timing issue that actually saves money is to rearrange the schedule of your reception. Since your photo experts are on the clock and charging by the hour, you can get all those special dances done and photographed at the beginning of the reception and *then* cut your cake right at the start. Your photographer now has all the vital moments captured for posterity, can take a few dancing shots, and then he's outta there two or three hours early. It's a waste of money to have your photographer wandering around the dance floor snapping pictures at several hundred dollars an hour. So rearrange the traditional timing of the cake cut and the garter toss, and then wave your photo experts good-bye. The guests can take over with their cameras.

Background Footage

Don't forget the possibility of displaying videotaped footage at your cocktail hour or during your reception. Some entertainment-savvy couples set television monitors around the room and arrange to have either footage of themselves played, or fun décor graphics like fish tanks, waterfalls, hang gliding, or other theme-appropriate scenery running in the background. Couples with money to burn have set up plasma television screens behind their bands and displayed anything from an underwater seascape to those waterfalls, or moving computer graphics for a little something extra going on in the room.

Placing Your Order

Once you've discussed the specifics with your photographer and videographer, chosen your footage and picture wish list, and negotiated your way into some freebies in your packages, get those items in writing. Make sure you specify what the expert is supposed to wear (e.g., a tux or dark suit so he'll fit in with your guests), the exact time and place where he is to show up, the day's itinerary, how many pictures you want taken, and when the final pictures and video will be delivered. Signing a rock-solid contract is the way to go, because you are hiring these people for very important investments. Some couples are devastated when their pictures don't come out, and they depend on their wedding insurance to pay for a reconvening of their bridal parties and families just for a second round of picture-taking in a wedding reenactment. It does happen. That's how important your pictures can be.

Candids and Digital Pictures

It's now common to find one-time-use cameras on each guest table with a note from the bride and groom asking the guests to take pictures throughout the event. Once the champagne starts flowing, you can count on getting some great shots from your partying guests (and yes, you can expect at least one down-the-pants shot from your buddies). Most of the couples I spoke to said that with the exception of that down-the-pants shot, they got the best pictures of the night from their guests' throwaway cameras. So don't miss the opportunity to get fun shots from your party that your professional photo experts *didn't* get. Something great might have been going on at table 12 while you were cutting the cake.

Money-Saver

For the best deal on those one-time-use cameras, steer clear of the wedding Web sites that sell bridal-decorated cameras, and go instead to the bulk warehouse stores like Costco and Sam's Club or craft stores. You'll often find the best prices there.

Your guests might bring along their own digital cameras. Do yourselves a favor and have a friend use your digital camera that day and night for great candid shots. After the wedding, you can download the images on your home computer and send them to a great online picture-developing site like Ofoto (www.ofoto.com) for prints that cost just a few cents each.

And don't forget to bring a camera along on the honeymoon. You can use your own camera or any one of the one-time-use cameras like those that take panoramic or underwater shots. I love the underwater cameras for those great scuba diving pictures, the underwater kiss, or the two of you swimming with the dolphins. You don't want to miss shots like that, and they will surely become the best part of your honeymoon memory books. Well, almost.

14

◇ ◇ ◇

What's on the Menu?

CRUDITÉS, petit fours, foie gras, caviar on endive sections, marinated artichoke hearts. . . . *Now come on, are your buddies going to eat any of this stuff?* When I talk to lesser-involved grooms about what's planned for their reception menus, many of them roll their eyes and complain about the "girly food" their brides have selected. Overall, these real men want a big, juicy steak on the list.

Here's where you get your say in the food, desserts, and drinks list for your reception.

Matching Your Menu

The menu you choose is going to have to match the style of your reception. So, obviously, your dessert and champagne reception menu is going to be a lot different (and a lot sweeter) than your full-blown, sit-down, five-course-dinner menu. You'll choose appropriate tasty dishes for each part of your reception, whether it's a five-stop traveling reception or the more traditional cocktail hour buffet and then dinner. To get you thinking (and salivating), here are some basic tips for your menu choices:

- *Match your menu to the formality of the occasion:* For an ultraformal reception, you'll choose higher-end foods like a raw seafood bar, some caviar, and perhaps filet mignon or other upscale dishes. For an informal backyard cookout, you've got ribs, steaks, lobsters, and salads. Your beach wedding clambake could have you dishing up clams on the halfshell, king crab legs, lobsters (again), corn on the cob, shrimp skewers, and the like. The menu needs to work with the theme of your party.
- *Go seasonal:* Especially with seafood, going for the more inexpensive seasonal choices is a good deal. Talk with your caterer to find out which kinds of meats are in season at the time of your wedding—that trendy Australian lamb could be a great buy.
- *Watch the weather:* If you'll be outdoors, select more cold foods to keep your guests from getting overheated.
- *Make it easy to eat:* Cocktail hour and buffet receptions mean people are going to be munching while mingling. So keep it to finger food and avoid foods that require cutting.
- *Include some low-carb, low-fat, and vegetarian foods:* Your health-conscious or vegetarian guests will appreciate it. It's a major no-no to provide food only for the carnivores.

Using Your Culinary Expertise

Every caterer and wedding coordinator I spoke to said that today's grooms are very educated and selective when it comes to their food (and drink). You men have traveled the world, sampled great cuisine, and know your stuff. Maybe you've been cooking for yourself for years; maybe you eat at great restaurants more often than at Wendy's. You can steam, sauté, and sauce better than you can grill, so your refined tastes can come into play here. In today's wedding-planning world the men are just as choosy about what goes on the menu as the ladies. So if you're a "foodie," speak up now, or agree by default to foods that might not cut it for you.

Trends in Wedding Menus

If there's one area in wedding celebrations that has recently improved across the board, it's the food. In years past, you had a choice between pasta, a stuffed chicken breast (probably freezer-burned), or medallions of beef with a mushroom sauce, green beans, and carrots. In the eighties and nineties, salmon started moving in as the entrée of choice. Now reception menus have gone global. It's all about international fare, frequently with a nod to the couple's ethnic background(s). You're going to see a lot more Latin food on cocktail hour and dinner menus (empanadas, mini-quesadillas, and so on) as well as Asian dishes (sushi and teriyaki). Caterers tell me that they're preparing more Moroccan-themed menus than ever before, as well as Hawaiian luau foods, true Italian dinners, and even weaving together fusion menus like Asian *and* Cuban for multicultural marriage celebrations. So with the global door swung wide open, you and your bride can look at great cuisine from around the world, as a way to mix up your wedding menu with great, unique tastes and maybe even a tribute to countries you visited together.

Another hot trend is food stations. Whether for the cocktail hour alone, for a traveling dinner reception, or as alternatives to the table-served entrées, you can arrange to have food stations set around the room for additional menu options. You might offer a pasta bar with three different kinds of pastas and three different kinds of sauces (marinara, alfredo, and pesto); a Cajun bar with crawfish etouffée and jambalaya; a sushi bar; and even a kid's food bar with mini-pizzas, fries, and hot dogs. Guests love being able to wander around and choose from a wide assortment of foods they don't get every day, so look at this option as a way to wow your guests.

Make Your Guests Hot

Not with chili peppers, but with aphrodisiacs. This is another growing trend in receptions these days, and probably one your guests won't even notice until later that evening. So go for the oysters, artichokes, avocados, strawberries, chocolate, and honey somewhere in your menu. It's the gift you give yourselves as well.

It's all about being different—different from your friends' wedding receptions and different from your parents' wedding. And what do guests remember most about weddings they've been to? The food. Especially if it's really good food (and also if it's really bad food). So give them something to remember. Reflect your good taste and culinary smarts.

Is Emeril Available?

You probably won't be able to get Emeril to come cook for your wedding, so you'll need to look for and hire a great caterer or chef to work his or her magic on your wedding menu. Chefs love to dream up mouth-watering food combinations for your wedding's theme, line up amazing dishes for your cocktail hour and dinner, and work with the new trends and seasonal cuisine to build masterpieces out of simple menu elements. Give a great chef a chicken breast, some wine, and a few slices of cheese, and a fabulous dish can result. Knowing what kind of magic the best chefs and caterers can work even with low-budget menu choices (like chicken and pasta, rather than filet mignon or lobster tails), you're best led to your final menu with the help of a pro.

What a Chef Can Do

At your interview, the caterer or chef will ask you plenty of questions about the style, formality, and location of your wedding, as well as your theme, your heritage, your favorite tastes in foods. Good chefs know to build your reception menu around what *you* like to eat. Sure, it's about pleasing the guests, but the food has to be all about you. Then, he or she will either pull out a printout of selections or load up a "Choose three from there and five from here" worksheet on the computer, whereby you and your bride will surf through the list of choices. So you might be reading off things like "Oysters Rockefeller," "Bacon-wrapped scallops," "Mini phyllo pastries stuffed with mushrooms, goat cheese and chilis," "Jalapeños stuffed with cream cheese and caviar." And yes, you can probably even have a chef class up some pigs in a blanket by providing a horseradish dipping sauce with chives. Great chefs can do that, too.

How Do You Choose?

Surfing through menu options and having to choose just a handful from the lengthy list of possibilities is the hard part. The easy part is *tasting them*. That's the best part of this job and probably why so many grooms are only too happy to accompany their brides to interview caterers: free food. The better caterers will invite you in for your meet-and-greet and then feed you. You'll get samples of their appetizers and entrées, perhaps even desserts. You'll chomp your way through a dozen hors d'oeuvre samples, then pick at some marinated beef, Cajun fried shrimp, smoked salmon, cod fillets, lamb . . . just to get a taste of what that chef can do.

The way to a man's decision is through his stomach, and many

> ## What to Watch For
>
> Always state your budget at the outset, and only work with a caterer who will respect this. Paying for the reception is the wedding expense that will require the biggest chunk of change. Always ask the caterer how he or she can make your budget work with the choices available to make it *look* and *taste* like you spent even more. You might be surprised at how a less expensive item can be made to seem high-priced. Caterers love the challenge.

potential caterers are going to feed you like your mom after she hasn't seen you for a while. So be hungry when you go.

At this point, you're looking to see if you'll hire this caterer and also at the available dishes. Once you find your match—the best caterer with the best menu options—you're golden. You'll work with this person to coordinate great food choices for your reception menu.

Looks like you have a match? Now you have to get into the background. Here are some questions to ask your caterer. This person is one of the most important experts you're hiring for the day, after all. Remember, the food makes the party. So be sure you're about to sign on the dotted line with someone who knows how to dish it up:

1. How many years of experience do you have in cooking for *weddings or large special events*? (Some chefs who cook for smaller parties might find your two hundred+ guest list beyond their capabilities.)

2. Where did you get your training, and when did you graduate from culinary school?

3. Do you belong to a professional chef's or caterer's association?

4. What is your specialty when it comes to the menus you create? (Some chefs have a particular flair for seafood or ethnic dishes. If your wedding theme requires Latin food, choose a caterer who's passionate and well-practiced in the style.)

5. How many assistants will be cooking with you on the wedding day? (Important for budget and space reasons.)

6. How many servers will you provide? (Also important, since these are the tuxedoed servers who will mingle through your crowd with their silver platters of hors d'eouvres, cruising by plenty of times with those stuffed mushroom caps and champagne flutes.)

7. Who do you hire as servers? (Most caterers use their apprentices, men and women who are learning the trade of wedding planning from the ground floor. If your caterer hires high school kids, think twice.)

8. What will your servers be wearing? (You'll want them dressed formally for your formal wedding.)

9. How much cooking space do you require on the day? (Chefs and caterers will ask you about the kitchen or tent where they'll be working their magic, and they might require a pre-wedding visit to independent, non-ballroom sites to check out the facilities.)

10. Will we need to rent anything for your use? (If you're creating your own reception site, such as at an outdoor wedding, they might want a refrigerator unit. Most caterers do provide all their own equipment, but this is one thing you should ask.)

11. Do you have insurance? (*So* important! See the document.)

12. Do you have a clean bill from health and food inspectors? (Again, *so* important! See that document, too, and don't hire any caterer unless he or she has been thoroughly inspected.)

13. What are your price packages, and what's included in each?

14. Do you have a budget package, and what's included in that one?
15. Do you have a refund/cancellation policy?

As always, it's up to you to read the contract fully, get every choice you're making listed on your official order form and contract, specify the times at which the caterer will need to arrive and stay on call, and note all the other working details in print. Pay your deposit with a credit card, and keep a copy of the contract. Call a week or two before the wedding to confirm that all is going as planned, and be ready for last-minute changes to your menu. Sometimes seasonal or market fluctuations can make that tilapia hard to come by, so your caterer might want to suggest another fish dish or meat alternative.

The Cake

Aside from medium-rare meat, grooms are also choosy about the wedding cake. Yes, the cake is a confection designed to fit the bride's wedding dreams with all those flowers and piped-on icing pearls. But it's also the closer to your reception and the focal point at your site. Everyone cruises by to take a look at the cake, so it's up to you to speak up if you have any preferences about its design and taste.

I spoke with several wedding cake designers recently—Sylvia Weinstock and Ron-Ben Israel are renowned wedding cake masters in New York City, and both tell me that grooms are coming in with their brides in greater numbers, with plenty to say about what their cake is going to be like. The biggest trend in the cake decision is choosing flavors that remind the couple of childhood. From their favorite ice creams, candy bars, pies, and other desserts, they want the same homelike tastes in their wedding cakes. So you'll find cakes that have been custom-designed to taste like a Mounds Bar or Ben and Jerry's Cherry Garcia. You'll find exotic tastes like a mandarin orange buttercream filling to go with an Asian-inspired reception menu. Crunchy candies are going into the mix, and cakes are even getting an overhaul to be 100 percent chocolate or they're getting liquored up with rum. Now, your individual culinary tastes in desserts can be incorporated into your wedding cake.

The bakers will feed you too. Be sure to stop in with the bride at bakeries and cake-design studios for the free tastings and wolf down a half-dozen sample cake chunks.

As for the design, the bride might put her foot down about wanting those fresh or sugar-paste flowers cascading off the tiers of the cake. She might want the ribbon that encircles the layers, roses, and piped-on icing to match the design of the lace on her gown. You probably don't care much about icing designs, but you should know that one of the most popular styles uses your monogrammed initials on the cake.

As for the cake topper, forget about the plastic bride and groom. Now, you can get more original and even work with the theme of your wedding. Some couples at beach weddings will put clean starfish on their cakes. Brides love the look of fresh flowers on top and spiraling down the sides. If your wedding will be themed, you might want to use something fun that the baker can design, such as a molded chocolate heart, a spun-sugar accent, and white chocolate daisies. I've seen some more informal weddings where the couple trumpeted their mutual love of pro football (they met at a game and attended the play-offs together) by topping their cake with two mini-football helmets. Giants for her; Cowboys for him. Some couples add their university flags, or the flags of their ancestral homelands/countries of origin, and lately it's becoming a big thing to use mini-American flags, especially at Fourth of July weddings. Toppers are fun these days, so see what's available.

The Groom's Cake

If you'll go with this traditional side cake that's served in addition to the wedding cake, you should know that this one is designed especially for you. Bakers will ask what you do for a living, what your passion is, your favorite sport . . . all to create a custom-designed cake that reflects your personality. So if you're a basketball fan, your groom's cake might be shaped like a basketball. If you're a golf addict, it could be in the shape of a bag of golf clubs. You get the picture. The groom's cake is designed with you in mind, and you get to pick the filling. So make it fun and different from the wedding cake, to give your guests an equally tasty second choice.

The Desserts Table

In addition to the two big cakes, you might offer a table filled with additional desserts, like mousses piped into martini glasses, chocolate-covered strawberries, and lemon tartlets. Or you could go dramatic with a bananas flambé station, a crêpes station, a chocolate fondue station, or any of the other popular dessert features that make the final hours of the reception so sweet. Your guests have danced off the hors d'oeuvres from five hours ago, and now they want something special for dessert. Finish off their night in fine style.

Belly Up to the Bar

This might be another fun place for you to step in. Deciding on the bar menu may be right up your alley, so start with this rule: It's always going to be an open bar, never a cash bar. It's bad form to ask your guests to pay for their drinks or to tip the bartender. The tab is on you or on whomever is paying for the wedding.

Your part in the deal right now is deciding what's to be served and how much of it. Most site managers will allow you to decide on the types of wines, beers, and mixed drinks your bartenders will pour for the guests. You can decide if it's going to be top-shelf all the way, if you'll have a completely stocked bar with anything your guests will want, or if you'll limit the selection (and expense) by choosing a few wines, a few beers, and a few types of mixed drinks. You can decide if you'll nix the offering of shots, which you might want to consider if you (or your bride) think your buddies will get out of hand. Or the bridesmaids, since we all know the ladies can also pound down a few and get wild. You'll decide these options with the bar manager.

Reception site managers tell me they're impressed with just how well today's grooms know their wines and champagnes, not to mention the upscale style of mixed drinks they want on the table. You suave grooms out there have your preferences and you'd never drink wine out of a screw-top bottle. If you can name your favorite merlots, cabs, and shirazes, wonderful. If you need some help, start off at a good wine shop or at a hosted wine tasting to get a feel for your favorites. There's a big difference between serving an inexpensive bottle of wine and a cheap bottle of wine, and your guests *will* be able to tell the difference. So always go for quality . . . choose some possibilities and invite the bridal party over for an informal wine-tasting party at your place to choose the final vintages to serve at the reception.

On the Web

For a primer on wines, a list of which wines go with which types of foods, and also some new reviews of the top vintages out there arranged by price, visit the Wine Spectator site at www.winespectator.com. As for fun colorful mixed or frozen drink ideas, go to the Cocktail site at www.cocktail.com.

Some of the hottest drinks for wedding receptions include:

- Martinis
- Cosmopolitans
- Vodka tonics
- Gin and tonics
- Sidecars
- Jack and Coke (or rum and Coke)

- Margaritas
- Sake drinks (for Asian-themed weddings)
- International beers
- Mojitos (for Latin-inspired menus)

And don't forget juices for mixers, soft drinks, perhaps a punch, and lots of water and coffee. You can match drinks to the theme of your wedding, such as daiquiris for a beach wedding, or include your bride's favorite Tiffany blue martini. As for champagne, go for the best you can afford. Your guests shouldn't be toasting you with bubbly that makes them grimace and curl their toes.

If you'll supply your own drinks for an outdoor, at-home, or unique site, do your research ahead of time, talk to a bar manager, and then shop at a discount liquor store, remembering to get plenty of bags of ice. Especially at hot-weather weddings, ice is the one thing you're most likely to run out of. Get more liquor and wine rather than less, and plenty of water—it's better to be overstocked than understocked.

Money-Saver

Know what "corkage fees" are. That's a price you'll have to pay for each bottle of wine the bartenders uncork. Keep an eye on the bar close to the end of the evening to be sure the bartenders are pushing the open bottles and not opening new ones. All open bottles, even those that haven't been poured, go on your tab. And guess who might be taking those bottles into the back room to enjoy after your party? The bartenders. So appoint a sober friend to remind bartenders that corks stop popping an hour or two before the end of your party.

A Word About Water

If you're holding an outdoor or at-home wedding when the temperatures might be soaring, be *sure* to have plenty of ice-cold water on hand. When guests are hot, they'll crave ice water with lemon or lime, so look into having your cocktail-hour servers offer not just flutes of champagne at your open-air affair, but also ice water with a splash of color, a cherry, lemon slices, starfruit, or something else to give a plain glass of water an attractive kick. It might sound basic, but I want to underscore the importance of having water for guests' comfort. You might even choose to have pitchers of ice water on each table when it's really hot outside.

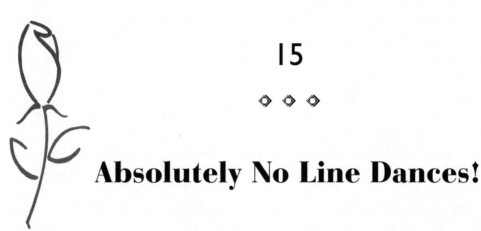

15

◇ ◇ ◇

Absolutely No Line Dances!

THAT GOES DOUBLE for the Chicken Dance, the Electric Slide, the Tush Push, or any other cheeseball line dance you've ever seen at any other wedding. Unless you're into that kind of thing . . .

Think back to the last *great* wedding you were at. What was the music like? Were guests out on the dance floor until all hours, singing the classics at the top of their lungs, pulling each other out onto the dance floor, working up a sweat? Were the slow songs the really *good* ones?

Now think back to the worst wedding you were at recently. Was the deejay in desperation mode trying to get *someone* out onto the dance floor and just not getting it that his retro-Euro music just wasn't cutting it for your crowd? Were guests suppressing giggles when he spun "Who Let the Dogs Out?" or used his way-too-excited voice to urge everyone out on the dance floor, only to have guests remain in their seats looking with pity at the poor guy. He might still be in therapy after that public humiliation.

What makes the reception—after the food, of course—is the *party*. And what's a party without music? High-level entertainment can make a good wedding *great*, and what you want is the party of your lifetime. You want a wedding your guests are going to remember and say "Hey, that was a great time" about. A party they're not going to want to leave. And you're going to want to enjoy every second, every song, every toast, every minute.

So if it's your responsibility to line up the entertainment for the reception, you have a very important job. The success of the party rests on your decisions. Not too much pressure, right?

Band or Deejay?

Either choice is fine, depending on whether you and your bride envision a great band playing at your wedding or a smooth deejay loading the original recordings of your favorite songs. Some couples are just band people. They want live music, and they wouldn't have it any other way. Others want the original recordings of the songs they love, no matter how great a band could perform them.

If you can't decide between the two options, you'll simply locate and audition several of both kinds of entertainers.

This audition is key. You want to see any potential entertainers in action, preferably a performance at a club or party, where you can see them interact with the crowd. Yes, many deejays and bands will be happy to send you a nicely edited performance video or CD-ROM, but you shouldn't make a decision based on what could be an old PR tool. The lead singer might have been replaced, the band might have changed its style, and you might not even be able to see the band through all the editing and special effects on some of those audition tapes. Go and see the group perform instead. That's the best way to gauge what they'll be like at *your* party.

Where do you find wedding singers and bands? Referrals are the first place to start. Ask recently married friends who they used and if they were happy with the act. Talk to wedding professionals to gather additional names, and surf through Web ads for local talent. Invest sufficient time and energy into this, since you're searching out the best performers available. Shortcuts could mean your reception will be plagued by the "Macarena," and a bad version at that. You don't need feedback from a poor sound system shattering the crystal and making your guests' fillings hurt.

Another reliable source is a local musician's union or a musician's association. Check out www.musicintheair.com as just one example of the kind of musician-finder site that can line you up with a handful of potential professionals.

The Interview

When you're interviewing and auditioning potential wedding party entertainers, you're looking for more than just how they sound on stage. You're looking for personality, professionalism, and a gut feeling that "Yes, I can definitely have these guys at my party." But there are also some finer details to get to, so ask each candidate the following questions, just to see if they'd really fit into your day:

1. How many weddings have you performed at? (You want a group or deejay with plenty of experience.)
2. Are you primarily a wedding performer, or are you more of a club performer? (This is *important!* You want someone who actually enjoys doing weddings and doesn't consider it just some money-making job that's beneath him. You don't want your performer to look bored, or your guests will be too.)
3. Can you play in our venue? (Some bands prefer not to play at outdoor weddings, for instance, because of damage to their instruments and general discomfort.)
4. Will you act as master of ceremonies? (Will the leader do the announcing of special dances, and so on?)
5. How many people are in your group? (The band leader should give you the head count, who the musicians are, what they play, what additional instruments they play for special solos, and so on. A deejay should tell you if he'll bring his assistant along. Remember that you have to feed these people too.)
6. Do you take requests from the crowd?
7. Will you take requests from us if we ask you to learn or buy a new song we'd like to hear at our reception?

8. Do you charge extra for special songs we request?

9. What will you wear to the wedding? Do you do a costume change halfway through to reflect the more lively party atmosphere after the dinner?

10. How much space will you need? (Very important! In smaller ballrooms and party rooms, the band might not be able to fit all of their equipment.)

11. How many breaks do you take? (Note: The usual scenario is to take a 10–15 minute break after each 45 minutes to an hour of performing.)

12. Can we negotiate the number and duration of your breaks?

13. How much time will you need to set up?

14. Do we need to rent anything for you? (Some deejays will require you to rent tables for him to put his equipment on.) Or do you bring everything you need?

15. What are your fees and overtime fees?

16. When are deposits and balances due?

17. What extras are available, such as a separate soloist who can do a few songs while the deejay takes a break? Light shows? Party props like inflatable guitars and glow-in-the-dark necklaces? What do these cost?

18. Do you have liability insurance?

19. What is your cancellation/refund policy?

Get *everything* in writing, from the song list to the amount of time the band agrees to play. Get the names of the band members and the name of the band, and put it in your contract that you are to be called if the band changes its style, members, the band name, or anything else. Don't be one of those couples whose band shows up as an entirely different emsemble from the one they auditioned a year earlier. Get contact information for the band leader or deejay and don't be afraid to call with extra requests or changes of your own. Pay with a credit card and confirm one or two weeks before the wedding.

Your Song List

Once you find *the band* or *the deejay*, it's time to compile your song list. Most entertainers will give you a sheet of the songs in their database or playlist, so go through and highlight songs you want . . . and songs you don't. Cross off those country songs if country is not your thing. And pencil in any songs you'd like the deejay to provide for you. You are allowed to make requests.

Time-Saver

For suggestions on the most popular first-dance and party songs at weddings, go to the following sites to cruise through their "most requested" lists:

- www.weddingchannel.com
- www.modernbride.com
- www.brides.com
- www.bridalguide.com

Just plug in "first dance songs" into their search engines and get their lists. Their message boards also may have additional song selections that diverge from/veer off the traditional path into jazz, reggae, instrumental, opera, and so on.

To get you started, here's a brainstorming worksheet for the initial "must play" suggestion sheet you'll give to your chosen entertainers. Just jot down the songs you know you want to hear and keep this page handy so you can write down others as they occur to you. Ask your bride for her playlist as well. . . .

Your band or deejay should let you know their specialties. In the world of wedding music, you can find musicians who specialize in certain song styles, ethnic music, jazz, and so on. Some groups just knock 'em dead with their Motown performances, complete with Temptations-like dance moves, and others can get a room swing-dancing while they toss their trumpets into the air and jump down into splits. Some groups feature a lead singer who's the spitting image of Frank Sinatra or Tony Bennett, with pipes to match. You have to see what your performers can do, and go the extra mile to hire singers and musicians who will give your crowd a *show*.

That's the difference between the best wedding entertainers of today and those of yesteryear. Outstanding "right now" musical acts know that it's all about the

- *Song for Our First Dance:* _____
- *Song for Bride's Dance with Father:* _____
- *Song for Groom's First Dance with Mother:* _____
- *Songs to Play During the Cocktail Hour:*
  (e.g., easy-listening songs, piano versions of songs, classical music, and so on)

  _____

  _____

  _____

- *Songs to Play During the Dinner Hour: (easy listening, slow songs, and so on)*

  _____

  _____

  _____

- *Songs to Play During the Party:* _____

  _____

  _____

  _____

  _____

- *Song to Play During the Cake-Cutting Ceremony:* _____
- *Song to Play During the Bouquet/Garter Toss:* _____
- *Songs to Wind Down the Party:* _____

  _____

- *The Last Spotlight Song We'll Dance to Before Our Getaway:* _____

  _____

- *Songs That Are NOT to Be Played: (such as your wedding song from your first
  marriage, or songs or artists you don't like)* _____

  _____

  _____

show. They know you don't just want *songs* . . . you want something to get the guests excited. So that's why you'll find deejays who also bring along a soloist to belt out a few live numbers. You'll find wedding musician *companies* who are happy to let you know about the hot salsa dancers you can hire to come do a group number at the start of your reception, or the flutists who can work your cocktail hour with class. You can get Irish step-dancers to open your party if your heritage calls for such a display. Anything goes if you've got the cash. And you'd better have *some* cash, because the entertainment is a big-bucks issue. After all, it does make or break your party. So consider this a wise investment in the success of your wedding celebration.

Making Introductions

As you're introduced into the banquet room, your deejay or band leader might be the one to announce you "for the first time anywhere as Mr. and Mrs. . . ." while your guests stand and applaud your entrance into the room. Smart couples make sure to provide their masters of ceremonies with a clearly printed list of names and titles for everyone in their bridal party and their parents, as these honored guests also get the big windup introduction into the room before you. To avoid embarrassment, spell out the more difficult names phonetically and take a second to meet with the emcee before introductions are made, just to be sure he has a handle on who's who. Some couples are now choosing to have the bride's brother, the groom's father, or someone else close to the couple do these honors and introduce everyone, since they're more likely to get the names right. They can even make the introductions funnier with anecdotes and personal information about each member of the party. This kind of personalization starts the party off better from the start.

Your First Dance

At the very opening of your reception, *you* are the entertainment. As you take your new wife's hand for that traditional first spin around the dance floor, you can either be a suave dancer and therefore great entertainment . . . or you could fall all over yourself with no rhythm at all and be (let's face it) probably *better* entertainment to your crowd! The pressure of the first dance if you're not a gifted dancer can make you stiffen up. That's one reason more couples are signing up for dance lessons a few weeks or months before their weddings. Just learning the basics of a waltz, salsa, tango, or two-step—and having a chance to practice with your bride—can give you the edge and maybe even surprise a few people. You should at least learn how to dip your bride without giving her a concussion! So let your bride know that you're willing to take a few lessons . . . and let her think you don't want to embarrass *her*. You know better.

Dancing with Your Mom

It's up to you if you even want to do this dance at all. Some couples are skipping the first dances with the father and the mother, and getting right to the group slow dances. If you do want to dance with your mom, your stepmom, your guardian, or a close mom-figure, then choose a song that works for you. "Wind Beneath My Wings" is probably the most popular, and most overdone, song for this dance, so why not go original with something a little more lively? No one said it has to be a slow dance, you know. And, to some grooms, dancing with their mothers to romantic songs is just creepy. So step it up! Get your dad and your siblings out there too. Make it a family dance, rather than a mom/son dance. Anything goes now. The same offer goes to your bride.

The First Toast

The best man traditionally proposes the first toast to the two of you. Hopefully, he'll prepare something short and to the point, sentimental and/or funny, and nothing that's going to get you in trouble with the bride. The best man's toast is the start of the sentimentality of the reception, and he might be followed up by the maid of honor's toast . . . since the women are rightfully taking the mike nowadays as well.

And then it might be your turn. Today, many brides and grooms are stealing the speech-light, stepping up to thank their parents for helping to plan the wedding, and saying a few words to one another. You'll get major points if you surprise your bride with a special toast to her, so keep that in mind, and consider sharing with the room. She'll remember that forever.

Flying Bouquets and Garters

The old traditions of tossing the bouquet to the screaming single women on the dance floor, and slithering that garter off your bride's leg to toss it to the bachelors out there, are going out of style. But you might want to be one of those couples who keeps the tradition alive. Either go the way it's always been, or add a twist. Your bride might hand her bouquet off to the couple who introduced the two of you, and your bride might want to slide her garter onto *your* leg for a laugh. (But please don't leave it there all night!)

Cutting the Cake

Another spotlight moment is when they wheel out that cake, and you both slice it and feed it to each other. You can:

A. Be polite and feed her a tiny piece of cake without ruining her lipstick
B. Be polite but marginally fun and feed her a tiny piece of cake without ruining her lipstick, but poke a small dot of icing onto her nose
C. Shove a handful of cake and icing onto her face before she does the same to you

Guess which one your crowd will probably enjoy more? As long as you don't lose a contact lens, and she doesn't get too much cake down the front of her dress, you're okay. Just speak with her right before the cake cutting to choose a game plan. Shoving cake in her face per option C, when she's expecting option A, could result in you spending your wedding night on the couch.

Tributes

Receptions are the perfect place for family tributes, so consider adding special all-group or select-group toasts. Dedicate songs to your parents, your grandparents, your friends, and your nieces and nephews. The more you personalize your reception and make it entertaining, the more of *you both* there will be in the event. And that's even more to celebrate.

Guest Interaction

Let your friend go up on stage and sing you a song if she's known for belting out an amazing tune. Let your dad play you a song on his guitar if you spent many a childhood night listening to him pick out tunes by the fireplace during summer blackouts. Put your brother on the band's drumset for a crowd-pleasing version of "Wipeout" if he's a drummer in his own right. Most bands are happy to let you request some guest interaction with them, and it makes for unforgettable wedding memories and priceless video footage. Some couples even rent the ol' karaoke machine for the later hours of the party—imagine both your fathers a little bit sloshed, arms around each others' shoulders, singing "My Way" together with cigars in their hands. Karaoke still has a place during the more laid-back hours of the reception and after-party, so don't rule it out. The bride and her friends could do a heart-thumping version of "Lady Marmalade" that could bring down the house. Remember, it's about the *show*.

III

The Big Moments

16

◇ ◇ ◇

Grand Gestures and Gifts

THIS IS YOUR TIME to be a world-class guy and show your appreciation and admiration for everyone from the bride to her mother, your mother, and your buddies. In this section, I've listed some sentimental gestures (from the *big* grand gestures to the smallest and most meaningful of gifts) you might want to consider to mark this special day, make your bride's heart beat a little faster, and get started on the right foot with your in-laws.

Because You Love Her

- Send the bride a romantic love letter on the morning of the wedding. Whether or not you are the mushy type, expressions of love from you will be *so* appreciated by her . . . and by everyone she reads your letter to at the beauty salon.
- Send the bride flowers on the morning of the wedding.
- Send the bride a small sentimental gift on the morning of the wedding, like that charm bracelet she was looking at during your last outing to the antique store.

- Send the bride the first item in your new family's collection. What better time to start your own tradition than now? So send her the first holiday ornament now, and get a new one on each of your future wedding anniversaries.

- Have a song dedicated to the bride on the radio station she listens to every morning.

- Call her on the cell phone and see how she's holding up. She's going to be very nervous as she's preparing for the day. Just hearing your voice could calm her down. Some couples talk up to twenty times on the morning of the wedding, so use those free weekend minutes you have.

- Give the bride a special gift from you right after the ceremony when you climb into the limo. It could be a diamond tennis bracelet or a heart locket. Steal that private moment between you—the only one you'll get that day, probably—and make it extra special.

- In the limo, propose a romantic toast to her, as another of your only private moments together.

- During your first dance, whisper the sweetest words ever . . . or the most suggestive.

- Propose a public toast to your bride during the reception, letting everyone know just how much you admire her strength, dedication, capacity for caring, generosity, intelligence, and talent. Watch her beam with delight and love for you.

- Get her an amazing wedding gift. Some grooms go all out at Tiffany, buying their brides that diamond necklace and earrings set she'll wear on the wedding day. Or, they might go with something outside of the jewelry world. Today's grooms are still ringing the romantic note while they also get their brides something *functional*. This isn't the time for a blender but rather the hammock she's been dreaming about buying, a new leather portfolio or briefcase for her job, tickets to the play or concert she's been dying to see, or first-class plane tickets for the honeymoon, rather than the coach ones she thinks you ordered. Or book the presidential suite at the hotel for your wedding night—make sure there's a great view, perhaps a Jacuzzi in the room, flower petals on the bed, and every other romantic fantasy she could dream up.

Because Your Mom Has Been There for You

- Send your mother flowers on the morning of the wedding. She's going to be a little emotional, and she'll love this expression of gratitude and love from you.
- Get your mother a special gift, like a diamond or gemstone pendant, a heart locket, a bracelet, a mother's ring with your birthstone in it . . . something she can wear in your honor and a rightful tip of the hat to the woman who gave you life.
- Write your mom a special note or send her a greeting card that gets the "thank you" words just right.
- Have a song played for your mom or parents at the reception.

That's My Dad

- Spend some time alone with your dad either the night before the wedding or on the morning of the wedding. Guys don't generally need gifts or expressive letters to get their points across—time spent together would work well. So take Dad out for six A.M. coffee, or go to the driving range for some buddy time.
- Have someone take a picture of you and your dad before you dress for the wedding. Bring in your brothers, too, for a guy group shot.

Her Family Is Your Family

- Send her mother flowers on the morning of the wedding, along with a thank-you note for raising the wonderful woman you're marrying.
- Give her mother a sentimental gift, like a silver heart bracelet or a heart locket. Have it be from the two of you, if you don't want to seem like too much of a suck-up.

- Give her parents a call the morning of the wedding to thank them for their help in planning the day and for being such a great influence on your bride. They'll *love* it that you took time out of your busy morning for this quick thank-you call.
- If they won't be hosting a bridal brunch, wake up early and drop off coffee and bagels or muffins at their house. Major points for you.

For Your Buddies

- Again, guys don't need Hallmark sentiments, although you might be able to find some funny greeting cards out there as a way to say thank you to your guys—especially if they've traveled a long way to get to your wedding.
- Time spent together is the way to show them your appreciation. Go for coffee, drinks, a round of golf, a minor league baseball game . . . something that gives you the kind of group time you've always enjoyed.
- As for gifts, look at personalized items you know they'll use: beer mugs, flasks, money clips, jackets, logo print hats. Even better, get them tickets to an event you'll all attend later in the year, like the U.S. Open, the Masters, a concert, or a trip to the Football Hall of Fame. Your buddies want to know they're not losing you to the world of marriage—hooking them up now with a great guy event is a way to let them know you're still with them.
- I love this idea . . . one recent groom dug through some old photo albums and found pictures of himself and his best friends when they were all just eight years old. He brought those photos to a restoration shop and had them digitally repaired, touched up, enlarged, and framed. Then he gave these pictures to his guy friends in dual frames alongside a current picture of all of them. The bride loved this image so much, she had it displayed at the wedding on the honored family table along with pictures of her parents' wedding, her grandparents' weddings, and other important family shots. Imagine how much the groom loved it that his bride considered his buddies to be family. . . .

Grand Gestures at the Wedding

- Arrange to have fireworks go off after the ceremony if you're taking nighttime vows, or after the reception. Just be sure to hire a reputable fireworks company and get all the necessary permits from your state and town—don't do this one on your own. It's hard to enjoy your honeymoon if you're newly missing some fingers.
- If you're marrying on the Fourth of July weekend, plan your wedding for a place that overlooks an already-planned township or city fireworks display.
- Surprise your bride by whisking her off in a *different* classic car than the one she arrived in, especially if she arrived by a less formal car because of the budget.
- Surprise everyone by having a special performance at the reception. While some grooms can afford to have celebrities play at their weddings, you might be fine with an opera soprano (her favorite music!) or a Doo Wop group to please her father (his favorite!).
- At a beach wedding, you might have a plane fly overhead trailing a sign that says, "I love you, [her name]" or "And they lived happily ever after!"
- A skywriter might spell out your initials in a heart over your outdoor garden wedding.
- A little bit of sneaky pre-planning and being in the right place at the right time might give your outdoor wedding some great scenery. Perhaps a yacht regatta and tall ships might be coming through the harbor where your reception is taking place or a balloon festival in the distance might have the sky decorated with colorful hot air balloons.
- How's this for a surprise? At an island beach wedding, one groom hired a scuba diver to emerge from the ocean carrying an oyster shell that held a beautiful pearl ring the groom had made for the bride.
- Scratch your names into the sand at your beach wedding, and have the photographer take a picture of it.
- Steal your bride away for some private time right after the ceremony. You might take a couple's walk along the beach, take off for the gardens

outside, or just sneak off into a separate room for a little bit of alone time.

- ◆ Arrange for a line of escorts after the ceremony. Not *those* kinds of escorts, but rather a lineup of police cars, fire trucks, military personnel, or anything else that works with your profession.
- ◆ Hire the local high school band to play the bride's favorite song as you emerge from the ceremony. One couple who met while they were both in the band in high school loved that throwback to their earlier days, and many of their bandmate guests enjoyed hearing "On Broadway" as an unexpected treat and a walk down memory lane.
- ◆ Hire trumpeters to play a regal announcement for when your bride is ready to walk down the aisle. You can go with pros, or hit up the high-school for performers in exchange for a donation to the band's trip fund.
- ◆ Have doves released after the ceremony.
- ◆ Have butterflies released after the ceremony . . . especially if she's a big butterfly fan or you had a date at a butterfly garden while you were dating. Show her you remember these things.
- ◆ Bring in guests your bride and her family didn't think could make it to the wedding. If you fly in the relatives from Naples, or the best friend the bride thought was working in Singapore, you're the hero of the day and you've given her the best present possible.

It's easy to come up with grand gestures on every budget level. All they require is thinking about what would thrill your bride and get your point across that your family and friends are extremely important to you. Go for the surprise, the grand gesture . . . because you only get one shot at your wedding day. And you can make unforgettable memories for the most important people in your life.

17

◇ ◇ ◇

The Wedding Weekend

You just read about creating amazing moments on the wedding day, for your bride, for your families, and for your guests' enjoyment. Here are ways to create even more.

Since we live in a global society—we move all over the country and the world for our careers, for love, and for personal enrichment—our friends and family don't all live in the same area. It might be years since we've seen our college roommates, our uncles and aunts, our cousins, our childhood friends. Maybe we haven't seen our friend's new baby yet . . . and she's three years old! Weddings are a time for everyone to come together for the first time in a long time, giving us much-valued togetherness once again. It takes something big to get the whole family to hop on planes and pile into cars for a reunion of sorts, and your wedding could bring everyone you love right to you for the *only* time in your life. But that one day of your wedding isn't enough time to catch up.

That's why more couples are expanding their wedding days into wedding *weekends*, planning a lineup of dinners and fun outings for all of their guests and family. If the wedding itself will be formal, which could mean that kids are not going to be invited, a separate wedding-weekend activity could be something the kids are involved in.

It's all about being with friends and family, since our post-9/11 world reminds us every day to spend as much time as we can with our loved ones. The wedding weekend gives you just that.

What's on the Schedule?

Fill the wedding-weekend itinerary with fun, *optional* activities that suit your guest list. Remember, your guests might have come a long way, so it's best if you give them the choice of attending the many outings and gatherings you might have planned for your three-day stint. Offer both formal and informal events, mix up the styles (a nice dinner out one day and then a laid-back barbecue the next), get your guests moving (à la a softball tournament), or give them the chance to tour your area if you live in a particularly notable, historic, or gorgeous town. Give them options for downtime (movies, time to spend at the hotel pool), opportunities to mix and mingle (like happy hour for the younger set), and provide plenty of kid-friendly activities like a trip to the arcade, time at a playground, or a laser-tag game. Mix it up and make this one fun weekend for everyone on your list.

Here are some of the most popular wedding-weekend activities:

It's All About the Food

- A cocktail hour at the hotel on the afternoon guests will be arriving. It could be in the hotel lobby, by the pool, or in a suite.
- A family-style dinner out
- A barbecue back at your place
- A picnic at the park
- A clambake on the beach or in your yard
- Dinner or lunch at a unique restaurant, like a fondue place, a Thai restaurant, or a sushi bar
- A dinner cruise
- Happy hour with free eats at the local sports bar. Guests can catch the big game as a part of your wedding weekend and not have to sneak to a TV to catch the score.
- Breakfasts and brunches, either at the hotel or out at a restaurant
- Four P.M. snacktimes or teas
- Outing for ice cream, gelato, Italian ices, or more gourmet desserts and coffees at a restaurant or sweets lounge

Active Outings

- Family sports tournaments, like softball, flag football, touch football, miniature golf. Make it His Side versus Her Side or the Men versus Women for more fun, and to get guests from both sides better acquainted.
- Morning or evening hiking, rollerblading, or biking outings
- Tennis games
- Tee times at the golf course
- Boating
- Bowling
- Backyard sports like swimming, bocce, horseshoes, and so on
- Adventure sports like mountain biking, snorkeling, or any others that might be available in your area or through your hotel at a destination wedding
- Nighttime or nature walking tours
- Biking by the ocean or along marked trails
- Horseback riding

For a Bit of Culture

- Group outings or individual tickets to local museums and art galleries (especially if there's a particularly interesting exhibition during that weekend)
- Tickets to plays or concerts
- Tickets to art house, foreign, or mainstream movies
- Tickets to the planetarium
- Free open-air performances such as at a town gazebo
- Street festivals planned for the weekend of your wedding
- Going dancing: ballroom, swing, or other
- A guided tour through the town's historic district
- A guided house and garden tour through your town or a nearby town
- Wine-tasting events

For Families with Kids

- Outdoor barbecues or picnics where the kids can run wild
- Trips to a local pizza parlor
- Going to the arcade
- Going bowling or playing miniature golf
- Tickets to the latest family-friendly movie or play
- A carnival-themed backyard barbecue with juggling, face-painting, and crafts
- Tickets to the circus in town
- A pool party
- Outings to area playgrounds
- Use of the hotel's or your home

- pool (with careful supervision, of course)
- Tickets to a kids' museum or a science museum with interactive exhibits
- Tickets to an aquarium
- Tickets to a sporting event, like a minor-league ballgame
- Planned kids' activities through the hotel's daycare program

You Are Invited . . .

Make sure you send out to all of your guests a printed itinerary for all of the events you have planned for your wedding weekend, and note whether dress will be casual, informal, semi-formal, or dressed-to-kill. Guests need this information so they can pack the right outfits and shoes to enable them to attend—and yes, guys also appreciate knowing that they'll need their golf pants for a round or their good black shoes for a night on the town.

Parents will be glad to know that there are going to be outings for the kids and that they'll get some time alone to hang out with the adults. And your single friends will enjoy the happy hour, dancing, and team sports on the schedule.

You know your guests. You know what would be fun for all of you to do together, so plan carefully now for a great weekend.

18

◇ ◇ ◇

The Bachelor Party: Before, During, and Handling the Aftermath

THEY CALL IT your last hurrah, but your bachelor party can be more about harassment than hurrahs if your bride freaks about what's going to happen, what *did* happen, and how hot the strippers were. Women have fantastic imaginations and can turn that trampy dancer who actually showed up at the party into a supermodel's hotter sister. Want a big fight with your bride? Go ahead and *mention* the bachelor party, and she just might explode.

Makes you wonder why you'd have a party at all, if your bride is just going to make your life a living hell over it.

So here's where you can start thinking not about the planning of the party—that's on the best men and the groomsmen—but how you're going to handle your bride after the fact. Silent treatments? Banishment to the couch? A sudden regression to no-sex-before-marriage? Grooms tell me their brides have gone to passive-aggressive extremes as punishment for attending their own bachelor parties and having a damn good time. Face it, she's not going to let it go. She's not going to ask you how it was, and take "Fine" as an answer. You, buddy, could be in for the third degree. Here are the *correct* answers for the inevitable interrogation:

- *She wasn't pretty at all.*
- *She was actually kind of sleazy.*
- *No, I didn't get a lap dance.*
- *No, I didn't have sex with her.*
- *Yes, I was drunk, but I didn't drive anywhere.*

What *not* to say? That's easy:

- *They got me twins!*
- *Can you get crotchless leather riding pants too?*
- *I don't remember what happened.*
- *Nothing happened.*

She won't go for that "nothing happened" answer. She wants the truth, and she wants you to tell her that everything she imagined didn't happen. She doesn't want to hear that you didn't get laid but your little brother had the time of his life. She doesn't want to hear about the stripper's implants, or the fact that there were *two* strippers enjoying each other. She doesn't want to think of you getting a lap dance, drinking any kind of liquor off of her or—God forbid—out of any indentation on her body. She doesn't want to hear that anyone else did that either, because she will hold a grudge and that guy will never touch your future children.

She doesn't want to hear about it . . . but she does. You'll never figure her out. But you should know your woman and know how she's going to handle the idea of your bachelor party as a whole. If she's incredibly secure with your relationship, she won't give a toss about your bachelor party because she knows you would never cheat on her. But few women can be that secure and that together when the wedding date is approaching. The smallest things can set her off either into tears or a rage, and throwing the whole leather-clad strippers thing on her is the official start of war. She might not think twice about the blonde she sees you checking out at a club (she knows you look, and she usually doesn't care because you're going home with her), but she can turn into a maniac when she's already pushed too far with a million different stresses. You need to keep that in mind.

And granted, she needs to keep in mind that this is your party, a rite of passage for guys, and it could be important to you to get out there with your friends and have fun. And she knows intellectually that if there's a real threat that you'll sleep with a hooker or stripper or some college co-ed from the bar, she shouldn't be marrying you anyway. It's the fact that *she doesn't know* what you saw or what you did that drives her nuts. And I assure you that what she dreams up is probably way better than what you experienced.

I asked a trusted guy friend of mine how you grooms can keep your brides from freaking out. His answer: You can't. It's going to happen, whether directly or indirectly. You just have to ride out the storm, tell her what she wants to know, and tell her you love her. Look her in the eye and show her she's the only one for you. And it couldn't hurt for you to tell her what a nastygram the stripper was.

What to Watch For

The morning after your bachelor party is *not* the time to send her flowers. She will immediately think this is a guilt present—you're giving her flowers because you did something heinous the previous night. She wants honesty, not presents, right now.

It's going to take a while for your bride to calm down. That's why smarter grooms and guys are planning the bachelor party for a few *weeks* before the wedding, not the night before. And brides applaud that move, since they don't want a too-hung-over groom standing across from them at the altar, or a groom who's still stuck out in Vegas because he missed his flight back the night before. It's hard for women to look at their grooms with love at the ceremony when they don't know where their hands have been. So urge your best man to choose a night weeks before the wedding so that you can take that bumpy ride through the aftermath way before the big day.

Even Though You're Not Planning . . .

Your buddies are planning the big night out. They're renting the limo or the bus, they're hiring the strippers, they're buying the beer and tequila. But you *can* step in and let your best man know if you have any preferences. Not just for blondes, brunettes, or redheads during the entertainment portion of the evening, but for the event itself. You might have been to a few (dozen) bachelor parties already, and you'll know what works and doesn't work for you. Some preemptive direction you might want to give them includes:

- *I'd rather the party come to me:* For some guys, hopping on and off a bus or in and out of a limo as you stop at every bar on the strip is just not the way to go. The traveling party is fine for some, but you might prefer to just hang out at one place and have everything happen there.
- *Don't get a hotel room:* If things get crazy, there could be damage to the hotel room, and the people in the next room could call the cops or hotel management. Plus, your bride will get exponentially more nervous about your being in a room with *beds* and strippers. Instead, have the guys rent a party room at a bar or restaurant, or have it at somebody's house.
- *Let's just go for a road trip:* You might not want the whole bar scene or strippers in the hotel room. For you, the ideal guys' night would just be a getaway to a golf resort, a casino, a car-race weekend, or the beach. It's not one night of debauchery, it's a weekend of low-grade relaxation and a good game.
- *Don't fly me anywhere:* Some guys will just bring the groom to the airport and fly everyone off to Vegas for the party. If you have strong feelings about not crossing state lines or dealing with plane schedules—especially if the wedding is just a few days away—let it be known.

It's pretty much unspoken and sacred that the best man is going to be your baby-sitter. If you're drunk out of your mind, he's not going to let you do anything stupid when things get out of hand at the party. And depending on who's on the guest list, it can get out of hand. So depend on your best man to watch your back, and let your bride know that your brother is going to keep you from making a jerk out of yourself. Depending on how much she trusts *him*, that could make her feel a little better.

ENDANGERED SPECIES

TAKE A GOOD LOOK AT JOHN CORCORAN IN THIS PHOTO...

BECAUSE YOU'LL NEVER SEE HIM IN THIS SETTING AGAIN.

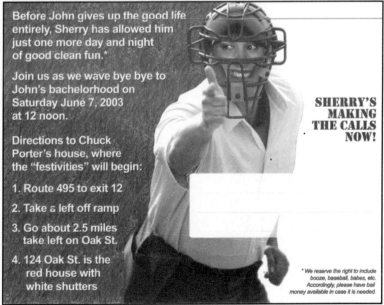

Before John gives up the good life entirely, Sherry has allowed him just one more day and night of good clean fun.*

Join us as we wave bye bye to John's bachelorhood on Saturday June 7, 2003 at 12 noon.

Directions to Chuck Porter's house, where the "festivities" will begin:

1. Route 495 to exit 12

2. Take a left off ramp

3. Go about 2.5 miles take left on Oak St.

4. 124 Oak St. is the red house with white shutters

SHERRY'S MAKING THE CALLS NOW!

* We reserve the right to include booze, baseball, babes, etc. Accordingly, please have bail money available in case it is needed.

Courtesy VistaPrint, www.vistaprint.com

225

What to Watch For

The first thing the men planning the party need to take into account is everyone's safety and well-being. Drunk driving is not an option, so they might rent a limousine or a party bus. If you hear that your guys aren't going to hire a safe ride, and they'll expect you all to travel that night, put your foot down about getting the car. With all the alcohol that's going to flow, no one needs to tempt fate or make any fatal mistakes. So feel free to let your best man know about the limousine company where you've hired your wedding-day transportation. It's a smart move to pass along that contact and potentially even help him to get a discount on the deal.

Getaway Bachelor Parties

Destination bachelor parties are growing in popularity, so consider the option of flying off to Vegas for gambling, Bermuda for golf, New Orleans for a wild time and great food. This gives you and your guys a few days together to get away from it all, kick back, and relax. This guy getaway is the perfect way to end your bachelor days and a more extended last hurrah. Plus, traveling in a group could get you terrific airfare and hotel rates.

Tamer Bachelor Parties

Some grooms aren't into the whole getting drunk and getting wild thing. It's not a good enough time for them, they're not big drinkers, and they'd rather not deal with their bride's attitude after the fact when the stripperfest isn't even their kind of party. Your buddies know you. They know if you'd prefer to go to a baseball game and rent out a VIP box for a great time. They know if you'd rather go for a golf weekend and have a few beers and a cigar after a good round, or have a guys' poker night at your place with some great chicken parmigiana sandwiches, pizza, and chips.

You need to know that more grooms are choosing the more sedate approach to the bachelor party, so it's fine for you to request that they tone down the skank factor. Here are some ideas for the non-bar, non-babe bachelor party:

- Going fishing, either deep sea or on a well-stocked lake
- Going skiing or snowboarding at a winter resort
- Going to a ranch for horseback riding
- Going white-water rafting or kayaking
- Going camping (Just don't watch *Deliverance* beforehand!)
- Going surfing or scuba diving
- Playing in a wiffle ball or softball tournament, or creating a new tournament of your own as an annual event your buddies will carry on
- Starting your own golf tournament, and traveling to get to a really amazing golf course that's way better than your county course
- Going to a casino or racetrack
- Spending the weekend on a yacht or schooner
- Renting a beach house for the weekend (Depending on where you are, that can be wild as well.)
- Going on a motorcycle tour with a group

The Morning After

Whatever it is you've done, and whatever the level of hangover you might have the next day, it's a wise move to call your bride as soon as possible. Let her know you're waking up alone, of course, and that although you had fun with the guys, you're still calling her first thing. You know how to melt her when she's a little bit icy with you. She might have had a rough night wondering what was going on with you. If you don't call early the next day, you're just lengthening the torture for her. So make the call, tell her you love her, and make plans to see her as soon as possible.

It's what you do, not what you say, that's going to lower the flame on her frustration, so take her out to breakfast, or go by her place and just spend the day with her. Be as sweet as always, as affectionate as possible, and tell her how glad you are that you're going to be with her from now on and not "out there" in the wild. Your bride may need a little extra tenderness right now, and your actions speak louder than words. Be attentive and romantic, and show her she's the only one on your mind.

And don't forget that the night before could have been *her* bachelorette party as well. Now aren't you curious as to what she did and saw last night? How were the male dancers' abs? Hmm? *You* might be the one who needs together time the next day.

The Inquisition Never Ends

A week later and she's *still* bringing it up? She's still pouting whenever the topic of bachelor parties arises or when a story on the nightly news even *mentions* strip clubs? Either chalk it up to her being stressed, or assure her for the fiftieth time that nothing bad happened at the party and that you love her. She just might need a little extra reassurance. But if she's being ridiculous about it, you'll have to put a stop to the topic. Look her in the eye, tell her you love her and would never do anything to jeopardize your relationship, and ask her if she doesn't trust you. Because that's something she needs to work out if your marriage is going to work. She can really lessen the odds if she's still hanging on to a grudge or if she seems to be enjoying guilt-tripping you.

It might just be that she needs to hear you say you love her. Because women who overthink things can really let their minds get away from them. She might be revisiting the topic out of fatigue, wedding stress, or true insecurity.

And keep your smart-ass friends from bringing up the bachelor party topic in front of her because it gives them a kick when *you* get in trouble with her. She doesn't need that. Most guys know to stick to the code and not discuss what happened that night. But you might have that one jerk of a friend who loves to torture you. If he's pushing her buttons, and yours, it's time to be the gentleman and ask him to cut it out—for her sake, and for yours.

IV

After the Wedding

19

◇ ◇ ◇

Planning the Honeymoon

YOU KNOW HOW to book vacations and plane reservations, so I won't explain the difference between Expedia.com and CheapTickets.com, choosing hotels for their amenities, packing for your trip, and getting a passport. You can find all that in one of my other books, *The New Honeymoon Planner*, and I know it's not going to be your first time out of your hometown.

What you *will* be working on is planning the honeymoon style and location. Many grooms love to partner up with their brides in arranging the honeymoon details and mapping out their post-wedding getaways. After all these months of planning, and especially after the wedding day itself, the two of you are going to escape into a different world together where you're not bride and groom, not your work personas, not anyone's son, brother, or friend. You're husband and wife, and this is your first vacation to kick off the new titles in style.

What Kind of Honeymoon Do You Want?

The most popular honeymoon getaway is of course the sun-soaked, island relax-fest, but more and more couples are getting away from the beach-only vacation and going for something exotic and adventurous. They're building their honeymoons around something they've never done before, like going scuba diving, taking a canopy tour in a rainforest, or going on safari. They're flying off to the Far East, crossing many time zones to get to Australia. They want to literally go to a whole new world and enjoy a culture different from their own. Big city tours, cruises—anything goes as long as there are plenty of *new* things to do, new tastes to experience, and romantic sights you can't see back home.

So here's where you start building your honeymoon. Ask yourselves these questions:

- *Do we want the traditional island honeymoon?*

- *Do we want to relax, or do we want to incorporate some adventurous outings like swimming with dolphins, climbing a mountain, biking down the side trails of a volcano?*

- *What destinations are our top choices?*

  *1.*_____

  *2.*_____

  *3.*_____

  *4.*_____

  *5.*_____

- *Do we mind traveling a far distance, or do we want to stick closer to home?*

- *Do we want to go international or stay in the U.S.?*

- *Do we want plenty of planned activities, or do we want to just kick back, relax, and go at our own pace?*

- *Do we want a cruise?*

- *Do we want plenty of nightlife, or do we want to go someplace more reserved?*

- *Do we want five-star all the way, or do we want to trade in luxury for more mobility and get to more places?*

- *Do we want great cuisine and great wines, or is the culinary thing secondary to us?*

- *Are there any activities we're dying to try that we can build our vacation around?*

For many couples, their budgets and the amount of vacation time they have put a pretty big qualifier on their honeymoon plans. Some exotic cruises can cost more than your wedding, and some two-week European tours at five-star hotels can cost more than the down payment for a house. As for time, what's your window of opportunity? Some people can only take a week off from work, and they're going to burn two of those days for the last-minute wedding prep.

The average couple spends a few thousand dollars and seven to ten days on their honeymoon. Hawaii is one of the most popular choices, followed by Bali, Belize, the Bahamas, Jamaica, St. Lucia, and other tropical destinations.

When I asked a group of soon-to-be-marrieds, their answers to "Where are you going?" ranged from the Seychelles to Thailand and Orlando, Florida. (Sometimes the dream getaway does include Disney.) Most of these couples said they wanted the royal treatment and plenty of excitement. They chose resorts that offered spa treatments on-site, for the bride who needs to de-stress and the groom who wouldn't mind a his-and-her massage on the beach at sunset. Waterfalls and tropical islands are big draws, as are the museums in London, wine country in Italy, and celebrity-soaked destinations such as St. Bart's and Monaco.

The world is your playground, so look outside the box to find a style of vacation and a destination that will give you plenty to look forward to right now, and plenty to look back on later.

Your First Planning Steps

Once you narrow the field, choose a handful of possible destinations and determine the following:

Will it be tourist season there at the time of the wedding? Do we want to be there in the off-season when things may be cheaper but there's not much going on?

What's the weather going to be like there at the time of our honeymoon?

Some islands might be in the middle of hurricane season, the hottest season, or bug season. So take your comfort and safety into consideration.

What's the political climate there? Obviously, you don't want to go someplace the State Department has just warned all Americans to stay away from, so check out any signs of civil unrest or danger to yourselves before you choose an international destination.

What's the price? This may be the clincher. That little island you can reserve for just the two of you might be exactly what you want, but can you swing $15,000 a night for it?

With any limitations determined, it's time for you to book. You could go the independent route and do it all through the Internet or through an individual resort's booking line. Some couples like to handle their travel plans themselves. Or, you could go to a travel agent for some expert assistance and perhaps a heads up on an even better resort or location. Travel agents may be familiar with many locales personally, so they can speak for the quality of the area, safety of tourists, and additional activities available.

Ask friends and family where they went on their last great vacation. I know I scratched a certain island off my travel list after my cousin complained of poverty-stricken areas all around the hotel and a barbed-wire fence being the only thing to keep gun-toting factions from showing up at the pool. Not romantic at all.

Explore your options. Check out www.travelandleisure.com to see hotels, cruise lines, islands, cuisines, and national and international destinations the readers of that magazine recommend in their World's Best survey. I use that great resource to choose my travel plans, since I know the well-traveled readers out there will only recommend the very best.

Read writeups in the newspaper travel section, surf some tourism Web sites, and thoroughly investigate any resort or destination you have in mind. Invest some serious time in this so that you can choose the perfect honeymoon spot.

Book far in advance. Nine months to a year is optimal, especially if you're marrying in peak wedding season when thousands of other couples marrying at the same time may have their eyes on Kapalua Bay in Hawaii, too. Look at honeymoon packages *and* non-honeymoon packages to see which gets you the best deal. Some honeymoon packages have plenty of free cocktail hours and a free bottle of champagne upon your arrival, but there's nothing in there about free tennis, free scuba, and free biking. Sometimes non-package deals can be a better buy.

If given the choice, go for all-inclusive resorts where you can eat and drink as much as you like, all for the one price you pay to stay there. No paying $12 for one mixed drink out by the pool or having to split a $30 entrée at dinner because you have to keep an eye on your cash. All-inclusives can be a better deal, and you'll spend about 25 percent less on your honeymoon if you choose this kind of deal or resort.

Look at travel insurance, especially if you'll travel during questionable weather seasons, on cruise ships that might be delayed or taken out of service due to a health scare, or if you're going someplace exotic. See what's covered and consider the relatively minor expense as money well spent to protect your honeymoon investment. Some types of trips just scream out for insurance, so think about it.

Look at what's going on in the area. Will it be spring break? Is there a big festival coming to the island, which can jack up all the prices and make the place a nonstop party zone?

Will you need to get passports? If so, apply as early as possible for them. They could take weeks to arrive and rush fees are pretty hefty.

Practice smart vacation-booking through reputable resorts; use credit cards of course, and see what your frequent flier or credit card points can get you for free. Some couples charge their weddings on their rewards-system credit cards, and then use the freebie points to book their honeymoon travel and hotel rooms for *free*.

Another option: you can register for your honeymoon through sites like HoneyLuna.com and TheBigDay.com. Rather than registering for toasters and blenders at a department store, you can have your guests kick in for your trip or for special outings, meals, and gifts to enhance your trip. Check out those sites to see if they'd work for you, and allow your friends and family to help pay for your big getaway.

Pack wisely and completely, remembering everything you need for dress-up nights, activities, and downtime. Be sure you have everything you need in the

On the Web

Check www.festivals.com to see what's planned for your destination at the time of your honeymoon.

way of toiletries, so that you don't have to spend $8 for one Tylenol at the gift shop. Bring plenty of film, batteries for your cameras, and enough birth control to last you twice the length of your stay.

You know the drill for vacations, both booking and preparing for them. So put your smart getaway strategies to use, and focus on enjoying your trip.

Make Any Destination Romantic

"Honey, I could have fun anywhere as long as I'm with you."
When you're with the right person, even a pretty lousy vacation can still leave you with smiles and great memories. But let's not imagine a lousy vacation right now. What I'd like you to do is see how you can improve upon perfection. How can you take that idyllic island resort and your beachfront bungalow there, that sunset outside your open windows, and that crystal blue ocean water, and make the whole thing even *better*? By creating romantic and seductive experiences, that's how.

Whether you're on that island or in a suite at a major city's hotel, on a cruise, or in a family resort, you can design incredible moments for your bride. Here are some ideas on how to make the most of your chosen vacation:

- *Enjoy your flight.* Flight attendants keep an eye out for mile-high-club wannabes, so indulge only if you're on a red-eye or a long international flight when patrols are less frequent. There's always a blanket for the two of you to snuggle under.
- *Decorate the room:* Surprise your bride by bringing along romantic props, such as massage oils, scented travel candles, bubble bath, and silk robes for the two of you. You can even request satin sheets from the hotel if that's your thing. Scatter rose petals on the bed and floor, and place a box of Godivas on the nightstand for midnight chocolate cravings.
- *Have the hotel prepare your room* with a bouquet of flowers, a tropical fruit platter, or a bottle of fine champagne for your arrival.
- *Bring along some seduction music* CDs for those romantic nights, or leave the windows open and listen to the crashing surf.

- *Schedule a his-and-hers massage* on the beach. Many resorts offer exotic massages; for example, using coconut-scented oils or rose petals, as well as hot-rock therapy. Expert massage therapists work your back while you enjoy unbeatable sunset views. You'll never be this relaxed again.
- *Take her to romantic fantasy spots.* Possibilities include huge waterfalls or a cliff where you can get a great view of the sunset. Helicopter tours over volcanos or sprawling cityscapes are also unique and memorable.
- *Reserve an enclosed underwater cavern* for your private use. In Bermuda, you can book an hour of uninterrupted swim time in an underground crystal-sparkling cavern that's lit from below to show the crystalized and sparkling stalactites and stalagmites; on other islands you can inner tube through crystalline tunnels to a secluded cavern underground.
- *Take a romantic tour.* Ask the concierge to recommend the best romantic scenery there is. One couple from Maryland said that the concierge hooked them up with a private horseback ride on the beach to a site where a beachside seafood dinner was set up for them under a canopied tent; a wait staff was waiting to serve them.
- *Give each other massages.* Read up or watch a CD-ROM on great massage techniques, and surprise her with your improved style.
- *Take great pictures*—not just of the scenery, but of how great she looks in the scenery.
- *Take great pictures during your alone time.* She'll love the seductive look you capture on her face as she lies in bed with the sheets covering her just so.
- *Leave her a love letter* for when she wakes up in the morning. Whether you're out for a jog or passed out next to her, she'll love finding your note over by the coffee maker.
- *Surprise her* later by writing out postcards to *yourselves* and mailing them to your home address while she's not around. When you get home, she'll find the mailbox filled with great messages from you, like "You are so adorable when you're sleeping" or "You looked hot in that red dress tonight."

- *Try exotic foods.* Even if they don't go over well, at least you have another shared experience. I still laugh over how the heads were left on the shrimp cocktail in Martinique . . . I love shrimp, but I don't want to see their faces. When my guy picked up a shrimp and made it dance across the plate, I laughed hysterically. I'll always remember it.
- *Lounge out.* There's nothing more romantic than spending quiet downtime or taking a nap in a hammock overlooking the ocean. That's bliss.
- *Pack her a surprise* . . . or one surprise for each day. You might get her a satin robe, a new camisole, a great book, a CD—some little surprise each day to show her you cared enough to pre-plan and you care enough to treat her to little surprises.
- *Keep an eye out for souvenirs,* and not shot glasses with the name of the hotel on them. Pick up a shell on the beach and save it to make her a necklace.
- *Book a private dinner cruise* on a yacht you can spend the night on.
- *Compliment her often.*
- *Feed each other breakfast* on the terrace at sunrise.
- *Go dancing.* Even if you're not a big dancer, tell her you just want to see her body move like that.
- *Have adventurous sex.* Bring a blanket to the beach in the middle of the night or get under that waterfall while no one's around and enjoy each other. How many people do you know who can say they scored in a rain forest or made love in five different countries in one week? Just don't take unnecessary risks. Mexican jail is not fun.
- *Sing to her.*
- *Shower with her.*
- *Watch her dress,* and let her watch you undress.
- *Make applying sunscreen more than just a skin-cancer prevention routine.* Apply it to each other every morning.
- *Draw her a bath,* throw in some rose petals, and then go out to buy her some flowers or a present. Let her enjoy some downtime while you make reservations for a great dinner out . . . or in.

- *Don't let the rain stop you.* Get out there and swim in the pool anyway, or go for a walk and get drenched. That's the perfect reason to go back to the room, shower together, and warm up.
- *Chocolate sauce is not just for desserts.* You can order chocolate sauce *pens* for edible body-writing—which I highly recommend.
- *Get a pack of temporary tattoos* and adorn each other, or surprise her with one that says "Yours" in just the right place.

You can come up with even more romantic escapades during your honeymoon than these ideas, so I encourage you to put some thought into planning seductive mornings, noons, nights, and midnights for your bride. This will be a trip you'll never forget, and imagine the stories she's going to tell *her friends* afterward. You are the man.

20

◇ ◇ ◇

Preparing for Marriage

I KNOW YOU DON'T take marriage lightly. No one in his right mind does. You're getting married because you love your fiancée, and you want to build a life with her that includes the kids, the house, and a lifetime of adventures. Perhaps you admire your parents' marriage, your siblings' marriages, your grandparents' marriages. You want kids, and you want to head up a happy family. And you take it all seriously.

As well you should. Today, 57.7 percent of marriages end in divorce, and you can find any number of reasons why. People marry too young. People are too quick to throw in the towel on a marriage that's challenging, rather than sticking with it and working it out. People whose parents divorced and are happier afterward might not fear divorce. And there's not the same social stigma over a failed marriage as in decades past. Whatever the cause, divorce is out there, and you don't want it near you.

So how do you act now to help keep the D-word out of your life? What can you do to prepare yourselves now for the future and anything it might bring, and keep your partnership strong throughout? It's a matter of not only preparing for the wedding right now but preparing for the *marriage*. Too many couples spend a year discussing centerpieces for the reception hall but not enough time discussing their views and wishes about marriage. Add in wedding stress, and some new marriages are rocky right from the start.

Having *The Talk*

Does any phrase make you cringe more than *We need to talk*? Usually, nothing good comes after that one.

But this time, it can. The smartest thing you can do is go to your bride, peel her away from that wedding-planning software, and say that phrase as a lead-in to a lengthy and relaxed discussion about how you want your marriage to be. Pour some wine, make a great dinner, lie together on the couch, and really get into the depths of your hopes for your marriage—even your fears. Talk about upcoming changes in your living situation if you haven't been living together already. Talk about finances, and whether you think you should get one joint bank account or credit card and still keep your own separate accounts as well.

Talk about raising kids. Which parenting styles do you admire? How do you feel about how people you know are raising their kids? Is spanking a no-go?

Keep any discussion open and positive. Listen. Don't argue. And don't see these conversation topics as arguments you have to "win." The key to a happy marriage is compromise and really hearing the other person. Pre-wedding classes as prescribed by some houses of worship were created to get couples talking about their values and preferences before the wedding, and even if that's not a part of your faith, it would be wise to open the door to a serious conversation.

Maybe you *don't* want a marriage like your parents'. You were miserable growing up in a house where you walked on eggshells, overheard fights, and endured silent treatments and taking sides. You don't want an up-and-down marriage, a stormy and dramatic conflict-based partnership.

And perhaps she doesn't want a too-traditional home where taking care of the house is "woman's work" and you handle all the finances.

It's important to discuss the models of marriage you've experienced in context with what you want your own to be.

You probably have your communication styles down by now, but you'll also need to look at how the two of you currently handle conflict. Over time, you've probably noticed that she stays quiet and thinks about something you've discussed for a while, then brings it up out of nowhere a few days later saying she was really angry. Meanwhile, you had no idea. That's one to discuss. She might need to trust you a little bit more, and you also might need to accept that she's just the type who wants to think things out from all angles before getting into it. The key is not to try to change each other to fit your way of dealing with conflict, but to alter your own styles a little to make things work out.

Lose the Baggage

If you had a messed-up childhood, or if you came from a family that was complicated, the best thing you can do in the interest of your marriage now is to work through those issues, lose the baggage, and work on unknotting those bad habits that came from your earlier family life. We all have issues, but some of the things we inherited from our families of origin just aren't working for us and need to be unloaded *before we bring the same kinds of troubles into our marriages*. It can happen without you realizing it unless you make a conscious effort to change, let go of grudges, accept, or learn new ways of dealing with conflicts.

Premarital counseling might be a good idea if you really have some dark issues in your past, or you might be the type who'd prefer self-help using a good book. The best one out there that I've seen is *It Ends With You: Grow Up and Out of Dysfunction*, by Dr. Tina Tessina, Ph.D. (New Page Books, February 2003). Work through this book and you'll undoubtedly clear away at least some of the old baggage you didn't even know you have. You'll step out of your old habits, take a good look at them in the light, and see if you're willing to bring unhealthy dealing skills into your new marriage. This book gives you new choices, worksheets, and solutions for a fresh start in your new life, not a repeat of your old one.

10 Keys to Prepping for Marriage

1. *Make your wife your top priority:* Work is important, but so is your marriage. When there are not enough hours in the day to get that marketing report done, make sure you take one hour to spend some time with her.

2. *Be loyal* to your marriage. That means not complaining to others about how she is or what she does while all the other guys are complaining about how their wives don't understand them.

3. *Expect peaks and valleys:* Every partnership has its highs and lows, so

when things naturally get a little flat or not so exciting, just ride it out and wait for that next peak.

4. *Be friends with each other:* It's not all about hard work, the schedule of household chores, finding a baby-sitter, and having someone to have sex with on a regular basis. Marriage should also be a friendship where you make each other laugh, you can open up to one another, and you bring out the best in each other and in yourselves as a team.

5. *Be affectionate:* Somehow, those little touches and surprise kisses you both gave one another so often in the beginning of your relationship seem to slack off when you've been together for a while. Don't get complacent. Touch her on the small of her back, hug her from behind, kiss her on the neck *just because.* It's these little acts of affection that women love. Keep her fueled with them and life is easier.

6. *Fight fair:* Couples who *don't* fight have larger problems than couples who do, so allow some healthy venting and arguments now and then. It's always best to clear the air, and if you fight fairly, you'll grow even closer. And make-up sex is always great.

7. *Be honest about money:* Money is a very powerful thing, and it's one of the most common issues married couples fight about. She spends too much, he saves too much, there's not enough, you don't balance the checkbook, she makes more than you do. Married couples need to be honest about their financial situation; share the job of tracking expenses, payments, and investments; and discuss potential financial decisions together. Keep your autonomy with separate banking accounts, but when it comes to joint accounts and shared expenses, you need to be true, full partners.

8. *Keep dating:* Plan special nights out and weekend getaways, and go out for breakfast together. Complacency is the death knell of any relationship, so always keep some kind of "date" with one another on the horizon. Surprises are extra credit.

9. *Keep your own interests:* Too much togetherness can be a problem if you slowly start to feel like you have no freedom and you're "losing

yourself" or losing time with friends. For both of you, keeping your own autonomy, going out and doing things separately, and even taking up new hobbies makes you both more interesting, content people. And no partnership is strong without both people feeling like whole individuals. If you start to feel too "blended" with one another, discuss how you'll both keep your individuality for the sake of being together.

10. *Look but don't touch:* I don't care how hot the new secretary is or how desirable women find you now that you're married . . . just don't fall into the infidelity trap. It's not worth hurting so many people, losing so much, and regretting so much after one stupid move. Avoid even the *appearance* of wrongdoing by making sure your wife meets any of your female co-workers, and don't run off into another room to talk to a female acquaintance on the phone. The shiny new toy is always going to be out there, and it can be exciting when a different woman thinks you're incredible . . . but you have something much better at home. Don't risk losing that over a hormonal rush and a severe lack of judgment. It's just not worth it. Cheating doesn't make you more of a man, it makes you less of one. So keep your integrity and decency, and always respect your marriage.

AUTHOR'S NOTE

THANK YOU for allowing me to help you through the process of planning your wedding. I wish you both all the best of luck, and a lifetime of happiness, laughter, and friendship together.

If you or your bride would like to share any of your own wedding stories with me, for possible inclusion in my next books, please visit my Web site at www.sharonnaylor.net.

All the best,

Sharon Naylor

Appendix I
Men's Wardrobe-Ordering Worksheet

Name: _____

Address: _____

Phone: _____

Cell Phone: _____

E-mail: _____

Tuxedo Designer and Style Number: _____

Size: _____

Shoe Size: _____

Accessories:

- ◆ Tie _____

- ◆ Cummerbund _____

- ◆ Vest _____

- ◆ Cufflinks _____

- ◆ Other: _____

Deposit Payment Amount and Date: _____

Size Card Received: _____

Final Payment Amount and Date: _____

Pickup Date: _____

Drop-off Date: _____

Appendix 2

Ring-Ordering Worksheet

Store Name: _____

Address: _____

Phone Number: _____

E-mail: _____

Web Site: _____

Contact Name: _____

Bride's Ring Style Number: _____   Groom's Ring Style Number: _____

Bride's Ring Specifics: _____   Groom's Ring Specifics: _____

Bride's Ring Size: _____   Groom's Ring Size: _____

Price: _____   Price: _____

Engraving: _____   Engraving: _____

Bride's Ring Appraisal: _____

Bride's Ring Insurance Policy Number: _____

Groom's Ring Appraisal: _____

Groom's Ring Insurance Policy Number: _____

Notes:

Appendix 3

Transportation Worksheet

Transportation Company: _____

Contact Name: _____

Address: _____

Phone: _____

Fax: _____

Cell Phone: _____

E-mail: _____

Car Make and Model: _____

# of cars booked: _____

Price Package: _____

Deposit Plan: _____

Paid with (Credit Card #): _____

Date of Booking and Deposit: _____

Pickup and Drop-off Schedule

Car #: _____

Location: _____

Contact Phone Number: _____

Time: _____

Who Is Being Picked Up: _____

Destination:_____

Car #: _____

Location: _____

Contact Phone Number: _____

Time: _____

Who Is Being Picked Up: _____

Destination: _____

Car #: _____

Location: _____

Contact Phone Number: _____

Time: _____

Who Is Being Picked Up: _____

Destination: _____

Car #: _____

Location: _____

Contact Phone Number: _____

Time: _____

Who Is Being Picked Up: _____

Destination: _____

Resources

(The following information is provided to help with research only. Neither the author nor the publisher endorses any company listed in the Resources section. At the time of publication, all phone numbers and Web sites were current. We apologize if any changes have been made by the time this book gets to you.)

Wedding-Planning Web Sites

Bridal Guide: www.bridalguide.com
Bride's: www.brides.com
The Knot: www.theknot.com
Modern Bride: www.modernbride.com
Martha Stewart Weddings:
    www.marthastewart.com

Wedding Channel:
    www.weddingchannel.com
Weddingpages: www.weddingpages.com
Wed Net: www.wednet.com
Specifically for You:
Grooms Online: www.groomsonline.com

Rings

American Gem Society: 800-346-8485,
    www.ags.org
Benchmark: 800-633-5950,
    www.benchmarkrings.com
Bianca: 213-622-7234, outside CA
    888-229-9229
    www.BiancaPlatinum.com

Blue Nile: 800-242-2728
    www.bluenile.com
Cartier: 800-CARTIER [227-8437],
    www.cartier.com
Christian Bauer: 800-228-3724,
    www.christianbauer.com
DeBeers: www.debeers.com

Diamond Trading Company:
www.adiamondisforever.com (site with
design-your-own-ring tool)
European Gemological Laboratory:
877-EGL-USA-1 [345-8721],
www.egl.co.za
Honora: 888-2HONORA [246-6672],
www.honora.com
Jeff Cooper Platinum: 888-522-6222,
www.jcplatinum.com
Keepsake Diamond Jewelry:
888-4-KEEPSAKE [453-3772]
Lazare Diamond:
www.lazarediamonds.com
Novell: 888-916-6835,
www.novelldesignstudio.com

OGI Wedding Bands Unlimited:
800-578-3846, www.ogi-ltd.com
Paul Klecka: 888-P-KLECKA [755-3272],
www.klecka.com
Rudolf Erdel Platinum:
800-RUDOLF8 [783-6538],
www.rudolferdel.com
Scott Kay Platinum: 800-487-4898,
www.scottkay.com
Tiffany: 800-843-3269, www.tiffany.com
Wedding Ring Hotline:
800-985-RING [7464],
www.weddingringhotline.com
Zales: 800-311-JEWEL [5393],
www.zales.com

Travel Web Sites

Tourism Offices

Tourism Office Worldwide Directory:
www.towd.com (locate and contact *any*
tourism department for states, countries,
islands, and cities across the world)

Discount Airfares

Air Fare: www.airfare.com
Cheap Fares: www.cheapfares.com
Cheap Tickets: www.cheaptickets.com
Discount Airfare: www.discount-airfare.com
Priceline: www.priceline.com
You Price It: www.youpriceit.com

Car Rental

AAA: 800-AAA-HELP [222-4357],
www.aaa.com
Alamo: 800-GOALAMO [462-5266],
www.goalamo.com
Auto Europe: 800-223-5555,
www.autoeurope.com
Avis: 800-230-4898 (U.S.), www.avis.com
Budget: 800-527-0700 (U.S.),
www.budget.com
Dollar: 800-800-3665, www.dollarcar.com
Enterprise: 800-736-8222,
www.enterprise.com

Hertz: 800-654-3131, www.hertz.com

National: 800-468-3334,
www.nationalcar.com

Thrifty: 800-847-4389, www.thrifty.com

Airlines

Aer Lingus (Ireland): 800-474-7424,
www.aerlingus.ie

Aeromexico: 800-237-6639,
www.aeromexico.com

Air Canada: 888-247-2262,
www.aircanada.ca

Air France: 800-237-2747,
www.airfrance.com

Air Jamaica: 800-523-5585,
www.airjamaica.com

Air New Zealand: 800-262-1234,
www.airnz.co.nz

Alaska Airlines: 800-426-0333,
www.alaskaair.com

Alitalia (Italy): 800-625-4825,
www.italiatour.com/alitalia.html

All Nippon Airways (Japan):
800-235-9262, www.fly-ana.com

ALM-Antillean Airways (Curaçao):
800-327-7197

Aloha Airlines: 800-367-5250,
www.alohaairlines.com

American Airlines: 800-433-7300,
www.americanair.com

America West Airlines: 800-2FLY-AWA
[235-9292], www.americawest.com

Austrian Airlines: 800-843-0002,
www.aua.com

British Airways: 800-AIRWAYS
[247-9297], www.british-airways.com

BWIA International (British West Indies):
800-538-2942, www.bwee.com

Cathay Pacific: 800-233-2742,
www.cathay-usa.com

Cayman Airways: 800-GCAYMAN
[422-9626], www.caymanairways.com

Continental Airlines: 800-523-3273,
www.flycontinental.com

Delta Airlines: 800-221-1212,
www.delta-air.com

Hawaiian Airlines: 800-367-5320,
www.hawaiianair.com

Iberia Airlines of Spain: 800-772-4642,
www.iberia.com/ingles

Icelandair: 800-223-5500,
www.icelandair.com

Japan Airlines: 800-525-3663,
www.japanair.com

Northwest KLM (Holland): 800-374-
7747, en.nederland.klm.com
www.klm.com/nl_en/index.jsp

Lacsa Airlines (Costa Rica): 800-948-3770,
www.centralamerica.com/cr/lacsa/lacsa.
htm

Lufthansa German Airlines: 800-399-
LUFT [5838], www.lufthansa-usa.com

Malaysia Airlines: 800-552-9264,
www.malaysia-airlines.com

Mexicana Airlines: 800-531-7921,
www.mexicana.com

Midway Airlines: 800-446-4392,
www.midwayair.com

Midwest Express Airlines: 800-452-2022,
www.midwestexpress.com

Northwest Airlines: 800-225-2525,
www.nwa.com

Olympic Airways (Greece): 800-223-1226,
www.olympic-airways.gr

Qantas Airlines (Australia): 800-227-4500,
www.qantas.com

Singapore Airlines: 800-742-3333,
www.singaporeair.com

South African Airways: 800-722-9675,
www.saa.co.za

Southwest Airlines: 800-435-9792,
www.southwest.com

Swiss International Air Lines:
1-877-359-7947, www.swiss.com

TAP Air Portugal: 800-221-7370,
www.tap-airportugal.com

Thai Airways International:
800-426-5204, www.thaiair.com

Trans World Airlines: 800-221-2000,
www.twa.com

United Airlines: 800-864-8331 (domestic);
800-538-2929 (international),
www.ual.com

US Airways: 800-428-4322,
www.usairways.com

Virgin Atlantic Airways: 800-862-8621,
www.virgin-atlantic.com

Cruises

Cruise Lines International Association:
www.cruising.org

Porthole Cruise Magazine:
www.porthole.com (find any cruise
line, specials, reviews, articles)

A Wedding For You: 800-929-4198,
www.aweddingforyou.com/cruise/cruise.
htm (weddings aboard cruise ships)

American Cruise Line (east coast from
Florida to Maine): 800-814-6880,
www.americancruiselines.com

Carnival Cruise Lines: 888-CARNIVAL
[227-6482], www.carnival.com

Celebrity Cruises: 800-722-5941,
www.celebrity-cruises.com

Cunard: 800-7CUNARD [728-6273],
www.cunardline.com

Delta Queen: 800-543-1949,
www.deltaqueen.com

Discount Cruises: 888-333-3116,
www.cruise.com

Disney Cruises: 800-951-3532,
www.disneycruise.com

Holland America: 877-724-5425,
www.hollandamerica.com

Norwegian Cruise Lines: 800-327-7030;
www.ncl.com

Princess Cruises: 800-PRINCESS
[774-6237], www.princess.com

Radisson Seven Seas Cruises:
877-505-5370, www.rssc.com

Royal Caribbean: 800-398-9819,
www.royalcaribbean.com

Train Travel

Amtrak: 800-872-7245, www.amtrak.com
Eurailpass: 866-9EURAIL, [938-7245],
www.eurail.com
Orient Express Hotels, Trains, and
Cruises: www.orient-express.com

Resorts

Beaches: 888-BEACHES [232-2437],
www.beaches.com
Club Med: 888-932-2582,
www.clubmed.com
Couples Resorts: 800-268-7537,
www.couples.com/03weddingF.htm
Disney: www.disneyweddings.com

Hilton Hotels: 800-774-1500,
www.hilton.com
Hyatt Hotels: 800-633-7313,
www.hyatt.com
Marriott Hotels: 888-236-2427,
www.marriott.com
Radisson: 888-201-1718,
www.radisson.com
Sandals: 888-SANDALS [726-3257],
www.sandals.com
Super Clubs: 800-GO-SUPER [467-8737],
www.superclubs.com
Swept Away: 800-268-7537,
www.couples.com/03weddingF.htm
Westin Hotels: 888-625-5144,
www.westin.com

Weather Sites

For checking the weather at your ceremony, reception, or honeymoon sites, including five to ten day forecasts, and weather bulletins for storms, tides, boating, and golf:

AccuWeather: www.accuweather.com
Rain or Shine: 5-day forecasts,
plus ski and boating conditions:
www.rainorshine.com

Sunset Time: (precise sunset time for any
day of the year) www.usno.navy.mil
[*Check this out if you're planning an
outdoor wedding and want to time
your ceremony for sunset!*]
Weather Channel: www.weather.com

Warehouse Stores

BJ's Wholesale Club: www.bjs.com
Costco: www.costco.com

Sam's Club: www.samsclub.com

Paper Supplies

(for printing programs, place cards, invitations, and so on)

OfficeMax: 800-283-7674,
 www.officemax.com
Paper Access: 800-727-3701,
 www.paperaccess.com
Paper Direct: 800-A-PAPERS [272-7377],
 www.paperdirect.com
Staples: 800-3STAPLE [378-2753],
 www.staples.com

USABride: 800-781-9129,
 www.usabrideweddings.com
Ultimate Wedding Store: 800-300-5587,
 www.ultimatewedding.com/store
Wedmart.com: 888-802-2229,
 www.wedmart.com

Index

◇ ◇ ◇